Soviet Politics 1917–1991

Soviet Politics

1917–1991

Mary McAuley

OXFORD UNIVERSITY PRESS
1992

Oxford University Press, Walton Street, Oxford OX2 6DP
Oxford New York Toronto
Delhi Bombay Calcutta Madras Karachi
Petaling Jaya Singapore Hong Kong Tokyo
Nairobi Dar es Salaam Cape Town
Melbourne Auckland
and associated companies in
Berlin Ibadan

Oxford is a trade mark of Oxford University Press

Published in the United States
by Oxford University Press, New York

British Library Cataloguing in Publication Data
Data available

Library of Congress Cataloging in Publication Data
McAuley, Mary.
Soviet politics 1917–1991/Mary McAuley.
p.   cm.
1. Soviet Union—Politics and government—1917–1991.   I. Title.
DK288.M42 1992   947.084—dc20   92-7517
ISBN 0-19-878066-4.
ISBN 0-19-878067-2 (pbk)

Typeset by BP Integraphics Ltd., Bath, Avon
Printed and bound in
Great Britain by Biddles Ltd.,
Guildford and King's Lynn

Preface

SINCE taking up a post at the University of Oxford in the autumn of 1985 I have given, each year, an introductory lecture course on Soviet politics since 1917. Each year, as the system I knew so well began to change its features, the task became more challenging and more exciting. To understand the present required not merely trying to keep up with events which, by the spring of 1991, were changing the political complexion of the country almost weekly, but also my rethinking the past. In September 1991, as I flew back from St Petersburg, the city where the Bolsheviks took power in 1917 and to which the heir to the Tsarist throne would shortly pay a visit, I set myself the task of trying to place the extraordinary developments since Gorbachev came to power in a historical perspective. The first-year lectures gave me an opportunity to do this, and to my audience I am grateful. Any student who flicks through this book in Blackwells will find a few more details, and some further thoughts in the Conclusion, but that is all.

In that autumn term of 1985, one of the first-year St Hilda's students said to me, 'We do like your lectures so much, all the other lecturers are so clever we can't understand a word they say.' Take heart, potential reader, I have tried to make the story intelligible and interesting, and I dedicate it to all the first-year students who, between 1985 and 1991, came and listened.

M. McA.

Oxford
February 1992

Contents

Introduction

IN January 1917 the Russian Empire stretched from Vladivostok in the east to Poland in the west, from the frozen Arctic Circle down to the arid lands of Central Asia. A population of roughly 125 million inhabited the huge continent, a population whose dominant group of Slavs, centred in Russia and the Ukraine, had spread out east and southwards to all parts of the Empire. More than 100 different nationalities—Armenians, Innuits, Germans, and Kazakhs, to name but a few—lived within its boundaries and, in terms of religion, Orthodox Russians were joined by Muslims in the south, Lutherans and Catholics in the west. Eighty per cent of the population were peasants, and illiterate. By the turn of the century, however, and certainly by January 1917, industry had made its appearance; the railways had spread their network across the country, large industrial centres and huge shipyards employed both skilled and raw unskilled labour, and modern technology was operating alongside wheelbarrows. The country was ruled by Tsar Nicholas II, whose brutal autocratic regime was supported by an aristocracy happier speaking French than Russian, by the army with its smart officer corps, and by the Russian Orthodox Church. Rule was carried out through the state bureaucracy centred in St Petersburg, the capital of the Empire, and in the provinces governors ruled with the help of the army, and new local government institutions.

In February 1917 Tsarism collapsed, brought down when the soldiers joined the women protesting in the bread queues. Nine months of turmoil followed. Revolution gathered speed as social and economic conflict deepened; an attempt to replace the old Tsarist autocratic regime with constitutional rule ended with the Bolsheviks taking power in the capital, and the revolution spread across the country. The Bolsheviks, a working-class party with a small group of intellectuals among its leadership, came to power in the major industrial centres with the support of the rank and file soldiers and the industrial workers. They, as a socialist party, were committed to replacing private ownership with social ownership, and to a society of equality run by workers and peasants, a society without coercion and without a legal system because crime would be no more. Freedom, creativity, and science would be its hallmarks, religion would fade away, and new forms of art and culture would emerge. A new international morality would inform the socialist world order from which war would disappear.

In Western eyes Russia in January 1917 was a primitive sleeping giant, a force to be reckoned with, a Great Power with whom alliances should be made, but a sadly illiberal regime who, it was hoped, might one day move towards a more enlightened form of government. With the coming to power of the Bolsheviks, Western opinion divided. The established governments were fearful: if Bolshevik aims were realized, it was the end of the system of power, privilege, and wealth which existed in Western society. This was a time when the upper classes were looking nervously over their shoulders at their own working classes as they too, began to claim their rights. In England wealthy members of society put their jewels in strong-boxes in Brighton so that they could move across the Channel to safer places should the revolution occur in London, Liverpool, or Manchester. The Western press portrayed the Bolsheviks as inhuman monsters, and stressed the Jewish origins of their leaders, and their unnatural ideas. But if unnatural, then came the argument that the ideals were unrealizable, and that here was a hopeless experiment bound to fail. This view was held initially by members of the old order inside Russia too. Very different was the response from the labour movement in the West, a response which resulted in a split within its ranks. Some saw the Bolsheviks as the standard-bearers of socialism and thereafter gave their support to the (Bolshevik) Communist Party in the Soviet Union; others were far more sceptical or hostile.

Let us now jump twenty years to November 1937. What did Russia look like in 1937 and what of the aims and hopes of 1917? A new Union of Soviet Socialist Republics had replaced the original Russian Empire, but it was still a single socialist state, ringed by a circle of hostile capitalist countries. Private ownership had gone. Whether we are talking of industry, now under nationalized state ownership, of retail trade and services, or of agriculture where collective (co-operative) and state farms had replaced family farms, private ownership of productive assets was no more. But far from withering away, the state had grown: a huge centralized state machine, consisting of commissariats (as the ministries were called)—for heavy industry, defence, education, justice—operated out of the new capital, Moscow. In place of that dream of popular participation, of an end to bureaucracy and hierarchy, there were state institutions, run on a hierarchical basis, issuing orders and instructions to the industrial enterprises and the institutions which themselves were organized on the basis of one-man management. The soviets, the councils elected by workers and peasants and soldiers, although they existed in name, had long ceased to be active bodies running local affairs. In 1935 a new Constitution was announced which gave pride of place to a legislature called the Supreme Soviet. On paper its provisions looked remarkably like those of a Western constitution: a federal system of eleven republics (each based on a key language group), with direct elections of deputies to the Supreme Soviet on the basis of universal suffrage. But the elections were not envisaged as elections between competing parties; rather the electorate turned out to cast their votes for a single candidate in each constituency, thus reaffirming their support for the order in which they were living, and the federal arrangements masked a system in which all key decisions, both on policy and personnel, were made in Moscow.

The key political institution in 1937 was the Communist Party and in particular its apparatus, an inner core of full-time party functionaries, directed from Moscow, and controlling all the republics. They were the ones with an authoritative voice, with the power to issue orders which were obligatory for all. By 1937, however, the party apparatus was under threat from the NKVD, the People's Commissariat for Internal Affairs, the secret police. The year 1937 saw the height of the Great Purges—terror, show trials, arrests of old Bolsheviks, of new commissars, members of the new élite, and of the general public. The Gulag, a network of labour camps, stretched across the country. And, standing above the Communist Party apparatus, the large state bureaucracy, and the NKVD, was the figure of Stalin, cloaked in an extraordinary cult of the wise leader—Stalin to whom hymns were sung, Stalin whose light burned in the little Kremlin window so that the citizens of Moscow would know that the great leader was always awake, always thinking and caring about them.

What though of society in 1937? Here the picture is a confusing one. On the one hand there was rapid social mobility: hundreds of thousands, even millions of peasants and industrial workers, of society's poor, had obtained an education and moved up to office-work, to positions of authority, and management. By 1937 there were factory directors who in 1917 had been apprentices, there were women who had escaped from the drudgery of home and sweat-shop, and become engineers, architects, doctors, and NKVD officials. This mobility, however, had been accompanied by a gradual reimposition, the reintroduction of hierarchy and privilege. By 1937 an élite had emerged with access to scarce goods, new apartments, and special shops. But this was only part of the picture. The campaign to collectivize the countryside from 1929 to 1932 had resulted in the deaths of millions of peasants, and millions more of the urban population were now in the camps. For some the 1930s meant achievement, a life their parents could never have dreamed of; for others, the old intellectuals, it was a time of confusion and anxiety; and for many of all strata it brought death in the labour camps.

Western attitudes were still divided between those who now saw the Soviet Union as the promised land and those who were more sceptical. For some everything that took place in Soviet Russia was good, a new civilization had taken root. But even their conservative opponents were much more positive than they had been twenty years earlier. The quality press referred approvingly to 'the sensible Mr. Stalin', who was perceived as greatly preferable to such heady and foolish Bolsheviks as Lenin and Trotsky. Mr Stalin had introduced a Constitution, brought Russia into the League of Nations, and, probably the most important factor, Russia was a potential bulwark against Fascism, and Hitler's Germany.

Forty years later takes us to 1977. In the intervening period the Second World War had devastated the western part of the country, and 20 million had died. From 1917 through to 1945 the whole period was one of trauma, of death, of tragedy, turmoil, and headlong speed. It was followed by an unprecedented period of peace, and social calm. By 1977 there were still 100 nationalities, speaking different languages, in a population of more than 260 million, of whom more than half now lived in towns. The old peasant society had yielded to an industrial one. In the previous twenty years, from 1957 to 1977, huge strides in education, in health, and housing had been made, and in the standard of living in general. Those years saw a rapid improvement in the provision of consumer durables and also in the food supply. But the pattern of provision did not reflect that found, even twenty years earlier, in the industrialized West. The Soviet Union still had a very large agricultural sector and a very inefficient one, short on skill and technology.

Lacking a transport system, lacking storage facilities, even a good harvest did not guarantee food in the shops. There were no super-markets, few cars, no shopping centres of the kind which dotted Europe and North America. It was still a society in which one sent jam made from berries picked in the forest through the post to relatives in other parts of the country who might not have any sugar in the winter. Industry had its advanced sectors, particularly in the military sphere, but also a pool of poorly qualified, unskilled labour, and by 1977 the technology gap with the West was no longer closing. This meant, for example, that a Soviet fridge might need seven times as much elec-tricity to run as its Western counterpart, that a pair of spectacles was twice as heavy to wear. In terms of quality, new products, and techno-logical performance, Soviet industry by 1977 was falling behind. The catching up process was slowing down. Militarily, however, by 1977 the Soviet Union had obtained parity with the United States: it was one of two superpowers. And not only that. It was now the dominant figure in the world Communist movement, flanked to the east by the Commu-nist Party states of Eastern Europe, to the west by the Chinese republic (albeit a difficult socialist relation), and courted by Third World coun-tries.

What kind of a political system existed in 1977? Political authority rested with the Communist Party of the Soviet Union: the single politi-cal party that was allowed, as stated in the new Constitution of 1977, to be the leading political organization in society. The General Secretary of the party, and also head of state, was Leonid Brezhnev, a cautious politician, who had made the Politburo, the leading party organ, into the cabinet of the system. This small body of leading party officials and ministers, chaired by the General Secretary, and staffed by the party Secretariat, took the key policy decisions. Thereafter the party appar-atus of full-time officials, stretching from the Secretariat down to the localities, was responsible for ensuring that the appropriate state insti-tutions executed the decisions emanating from the centre. The mass membership of the party now stood at approximately 16 million; many of its members' views were indistinguishable from those of non-members but they were obliged to carry out the instructions and de-cisions taken by the higher party organizations. Many worked, in different capacities, in the huge state apparatus which was growing visibly year by year, as ever more institutions, ministries, and state committees encrusted the overblown centre of the empire. Coercion was still there, but in the background rather than to the fore. The KGB was still responsible for surveillance and control but it was no longer operating a system of terror, of arbitrary arrest and repression. By 1977 citizens knew what was and was not permissible.

We are talking then of a highly centralized system of political control over all major activities, the economy, the media, and social activities. The key values of the system, by 1977, had become those of patriotism, stability, and order. As an example, let us take the initiation ceremony at which 9-year-old children joined the Young Pioneers, the youth organization. They would be given their red ties, their little badges of Lenin, and, during the ceremony, introduced to individuals who represented the heroes of Soviet society, past and present. The person they would have wished most of all to have present was, of course, Lenin. By then he was a sacred figure, the father figure, the person who had made the revolution and made life ever better for children not only in the Soviet Union but throughout the world. Given this was impossible, it was desirable to find an old Bolshevik, someone who had known Lenin, preferably someone who had touched him, at the least someone who had seen him and would be able to tell the children what he or she had thought and felt on hearing Lenin speak. A second individual would be a veteran of the Second World War, someone who had defended the motherland and who could talk of the fight against the fascists, and a third would be a hero of socialist labour, a worker with an outstanding production record. Ideally he or she would be a *young* hero of socialist labour whose father or mother and grandparents before that had worked in the same factory—the representative of a labour dynasty. Here then were three figures signifying the system: Lenin—the revolution; the war veteran—patriotism; and a hero of socialist labour—the working class.

Western attitudes were by now far more ambivalent, both those of the establishment and those within the labour movement. The Soviet Union had been an ally in the second World War, but then came the Cold War, and the spread of Communism throughout the world. In the 1950s the American public could still be swayed by anti-Communist hysteria, while Communist candidates won elections in Europe. But Khrushchev's denunciation of Stalin's dictatorship in 1956, the Soviet government's use of force in Hungary in 1956 and Czechoslovakia in 1968, and the United States' inability to portray, even to itself, the Vietnam war as a fight for freedom, made the old convictions less secure. The 1970s saw *détente* and new co-operation between the world's two great nuclear powers, but civil rights still dogged the agenda. As ideological passion gave way to cautious conservatism in the Soviet Union, so in the West defenders and critics voiced their convictions less stridently. The European Communist parties began to distance themselves from Moscow and when, in the 1980s, Ronald Reagan tried to re-create 'the evil empire' the theme had little resonance, even in the United States.

In 1988, as Reagan left the White House, the Soviet Union had an energetic new Communist Party leader, Mikhail Gorbachev, who was speaking out on the need for economic and political reform, but no major changes had yet taken place. Brezhnev, who died in 1982, would have disapproved of many of Gorbachev's statements, and counselled against such rash adventurism, but he would have recognized the system as the one he knew. By the end of 1991, within the space of three years, both his and Gorbachev's world had gone for ever, with momentous and unpredictable consequences not only for the peoples of the Soviet Union but for the world as a whole.

It was not simply that what had appeared to be a stable, authoritarian regime in an increasingly conservative society found itself forced to adapt to unexpected pressures for change, but that the political system fell apart, the empire disintegrated, and the economy collapsed. Even arrangements that had pre-dated the revolution of 1917 bit the dust. It was not just that the countries of Eastern Europe gained their independence, and the Baltic states which had been incorporated into the Soviet Union at the time of the Second World War became sovereign states, but that, on the territory of the original Russian Empire which had formed the basis for the subsequent Union of Soviet Socialist Republics, a new Commonwealth of sovereign states was announced. When the heir to the Tsarist throne, Grand Duke Vladimir, flew in from Paris in November 1991 for the celebrations to mark the renaming of Leningrad as St Petersburg, he arrived in a Russia which no longer ruled the Ukraine, Georgia, Armenia, and those lands of Central Asia which had belonged to his forefathers. These new sovereign states now had popularly elected parliaments or presidents, some of whom, such as Yeltsin in Russia and Kravchuk in the Ukraine were old Communist Party politicians, while others, such as Gamsakhurdia in Georgia (shortly to be ousted by force) or Landsbergis in Lithuania, were 'dissidents' or newcomers to politics. The Communist Party of the Soviet

Union had been dissolved, and its republican organizations banned in most republics.

As political authority had slipped away, during 1990 and 1991, from the central institutions to the republics, and the Communist Party lost its power and position, the centre had grown weaker and weaker. By August 1991 there was a black hole: a President with the power to issue decrees that were not implemented, left only with control over the still centralized means of coercion, the military, KGB, and Ministry of Internal Affairs, although the degree of central control over the latter two was already in doubt. An attempted coup by some of Gorbachev's ministers sought to reimpose some kind of control over a territory, the old Empire, in which central political authority had evaporated. With its failure the republican governments began, in keeping with their political autonomy, to claim the responsibility for the defence of their territories. The nakedness of the Presidency became all too apparent: the existence of the nuclear arsenal its only remaining rationale. By December 1991 both the Presidency and other central institutions had been wound up, and the question of who should control the armed forces came to the fore.

The breakneck political change was not accompanied by economic reform and, as the centrally planned economy broke down and failed to provide the goods, the central government printed more money and raised wages, while the economy spiralled ever downwards. With the abolition of the centre, the new republican governments became responsible for those resources that traditionally came under the jurisdiction of the central ministries, and for the worsening economic situation. All that had been agreed by the end of 1991, and to varying degrees by the different republican governments, was that state ownership and central planning must be replaced by some kind of a private-ownership market system if their economies were ever going to compete with the advanced industrial countries of east and west.

The key resources of the media were no longer centrally controlled, indeed they were hardly controlled at all. In liberal democratic systems the degree of state control and censorship varies, as does the control over editorial policy by those who own radio, television companies, and the press. But in the Soviet Union, as central government control began to slip, an extraordinary situation developed in which those who spoke for the media became responsible to no one but themselves. They still drew their salaries because the bureaucratic state machine still trundled on; the constraints were those of the availability of paper and of equipment, and the whims of producers, the journalists themselves, and, for local media, the local authorities. Soviet television became perhaps the freest medium in the world.

If 1917 saw a revolution that changed the face of the world for the next fifty years, 1989–91 witnessed a phenomenon of equal significance: the disintegration, in the space of three years, of probably the most powerful empire the world has known. The world Communist movement, the movement whose aim had been to bury capitalism, was no more. It is too early even to guess the repercussions. We suggested earlier that Western reactions to 1917, to Stalinism, and to the Soviet Union under Brezhnev had varied, and were strongly influenced by factors in the home environment. The reader might like to pause, and consider why the press and the politicians of the late 1980s adopted the positions they did towards the reform process, and the collapse of Communist Party rule. Are Western perceptions in 1990 any better informed than those of 1917, and what are the interests involved? A concern for democracy and human rights, or for strategic weapons and the balance of power in the world, fear of the repercussions of economic chaos, or the chance to plunder the rich resources of a huge continent? How will a future generation assess the West's reaction to the end of Communist Party rule? One thing is for certain: the collapse owed nothing to the politics of Western powers (technological progress was perhaps a different matter), but the continued support for the Gorbachev leadership may have accentuated the economic crisis and therefore contributed to the subsequent political instability.

Our aim is to try to make sense of the developments since 1985: to show how and why the system fell apart. This requires an understanding of the historical context of the drama, and of the Soviet political system, and also of the way in which, more generally, political change occurs. What is the relationship between economic development (or stagnation) and political change, if any? Do social change or cultural traditions influence political outcomes? Why *does* political change occur? Do key individuals play a part under some circumstances, and, if so, which? Explanations differ, sometimes dramatically.

How then should we begin? We want to arrive at a position from which we can analyse and understand recent and current political developments in what was the Soviet Union. It will help if we bear in mind certain key factors that are relevant to the establishment and maintenance of political regimes in the modern world. Politics, it is often said, is about the exercise of power within society. But such a statement is too broad: there are many kinds of power we would not want to describe as political. It is better to think in terms of a particular type of power: that associated with *ruling*, with the ability to determine the rules for a society, and to back up their implementation with force, if need be. Authority and control of the means of coercion are the key attributes of rulers. That does not mean that there are not instances when those in control possess nothing but their weapons, but this is an unstable basis for rule because the *right* to rule, the authority of those in power, is not recognized. Hence rulers are anxious to acquire authority, which may rest on different bases: it may, for example, be seen as God given, to stem from tradition, or from an election. This has the consequence that those who possess political power are always sharply observant of those who control the means of communication, of culture and education: in older times the Church, today the media and education. They may be content to observe, to intervene at the edges, if their authority is not threatened; they may move in to censor or take over. Similarly they will be concerned with the use of economic resources. If the rulers are to maintain an army to defend the territory against outsiders and order within it (perhaps their basic task), they need to raise taxes; they may also decide they require revenue to provide themselves with the lifestyle to which they feel entitled, or to carry out certain projects. Now a poor economy not only provides a weak tax base, but is likely to increase the discontent of those who have to pay. Hence economic prosperity is desirable, and even more desirable if the rulers acquire the obligation to provide education or welfare. They may well feel the need to strike a delicate balance between allowing those who own and dispose of the economic resources to exploit them as they wish, and ensuring that the consequences do not create a level of social discontent that jeopardizes their own safety as rulers. Hence those who control the political resources (authority and coercion) will be very aware of those who control economic resources and may, for different reasons, move in to share or limit the rights of ownership.

There are then resources which provide those who possess them with power: the means of coercion, the attribute of authority, control of knowledge and ideas, the ownership of economic resources. Control over the means of coercion is the most important because it will decide the outcome of an issue if it cannot be resolved by other means; it is the most powerful resource of all. In analysing political regimes we take that for granted, then turn our attention to the relationships between the holders of political office (and authority), the citizenry, and those who 'own' and control the other key resources. These will determine the key contours of the state–society relationship. Coercion, authority, economic resources, and the means of communication all featured in the thumb-nail sketches of 1917, 1937, 1977, and 1991, and the changing relationship between them will run like a motif through the following chapters.

If a major objective is to make sense of developments in the Soviet Union as *perestroika* turned into the collapse of Communist Party rule, the other is to cast light on the extraordinary period 1917–91 as a whole. There was a revolution, the creation of a new state, an unprecedented experiment at crash industrialization and social mobility, a dictatorship and mass terror, its replacement by a system of conservative state control, and then the swift collapse of the state, the end of empire, and embryonic attempts to create a new political order. All pose interesting and difficult problems of analysis in their own right. All raise important political issues. To mention but two: what are the causes and consequences of terror, and what are the pre-conditions for the establishment and maintenance of a democratic order? As we shall see, there are no easy answers. The chapters that follow, while providing a minimal narrative account of the political history of the period, each addresses a different and important political topic. We begin with revolution.

ONE

1917: Revolution

A REVOLUTION implies not just a change of government but a total breakdown of the system through which rulers govern a society, and a reordering of society itself. Usually this involves action, violent action, by sections of society. Society frees itself temporarily from any form of rule, hence the hallmarks of a revolution, of a revolutionary period, are freedom and violence. A struggle for power begins almost immediately, a struggle in which the ability to combine social action with control over the means of coercion becomes crucial, and in which new groups compete for possession of society's resources. Visions of a new order appear. Those who lead in the early stages are often swept away by more radical groups who come into existence as economic hardship and social turbulence increase. The year 1917 certainly qualifies as a year of revolution; whether 1991 does too is a question to return to at the end.

In January 1917 Russia was ruled by an autocratic Tsar, flanked by the nobility, supported by the army, sustained by the Church and the state bureaucracy. A year later the country had a Bolshevik government, a Council of People's Commissars, committed to the introduction of social ownership, a workers' government, and equality. Although, however, the Bolsheviks claimed to be the government, they were far from controlling or ruling the country: it would take a civil war before they could substantiate their claim. Supporters of the old order and of other political parties were prepared to defend their positions in 1918. The Tsar and his family were under house arrest, and shortly would be executed in the cellar of the house in Ekaterinburg in which they were being held. The nobility was leaving for Europe or the south where the Tsarist generals were putting together an army. Some of the officers had joined them, others sat at the cafe tables in St Petersburg (still the capital but renamed Petrograd in the early years of the war) plotting against the new Bolshevik government. The civil servants were on strike; the intelligentsia in disarray. The Bolsheviks' socialist opponents were regrouping. Meanwhile across the country the peasants were taking the land, industry was in crisis, the economy spinning ever downwards, and unemployment mounting in the major cities as the defence industries ground to a halt.

What happened in Russia in that extraordinary year of revolution? Before we trace the process itself, a reminder. Whether the topic is 1917, or any period in the subsequent history of Russia and the Soviet Union, very different and conflicting interpretations exist, be they those of the time or of later Western or Soviet historians. By way of example, let us contrast three different interpretations, albeit simplified, of what happened in 1917. All three have found support among significant groups of people at different times. We can call the first the constitutional view. This emphasizes that Russia, by the early twentieth century, was leaving its backward past behind; an urban and industrial infrastructure was developing, a professional middle class was emerging, and land reform was under way in the countryside. With more skilful and flexible political leaders, the argument runs, Russia could have passed relatively peacefully to some form of accountable constitutional government. Following the February revolution a democratic order could have been introduced and maintained had the leaders of the different political parties been prepared to work together. Unfortunately, the argument continues, the Bolsheviks, a dictatorial group, seized power and prevented this outcome.

A contrasting view, which we can call the class view, was advanced by the Bolsheviks at the time, and subsequently became the standard Soviet interpretation. This runs roughly as follows. The class conflict, inherent in a society where ownership of land and the means of production were concentrated in the hands of a few, was accentuated in Russia by the strains and stresses of the war, and the policies of a repressive government. It exploded in the revolutionary developments which took place from February on. The Bolsheviks were agents of an inevitable historical process in which capitalism yields to socialism, just as feudalism was superseded by capitalism, a more efficient productive order. By taking power in October the Bolsheviks were acting not merely on behalf of Russia's poor, whom they set on the path to progress and social equality, but of the international working class.

Now for a third view which, for want of a better word, we can call the cultural view. This emphasizes that Russia had a unique social and economic infrastructure, peasant based and Church rooted, with its own culture of authority and spirituality, very different from Western society and Western values, and that, therefore, Russia was and is endlessly searching for a form of government and society that can embody these values, cultural norms, and aspirations. In this perspective the revolution and its outcome was a disaster, the fault of both those who mistakenly sought to take Russia forward to a Western industrialized constitutional future and of the Bolsheviks with their Marxist notions. We shall return to these views, but now for the developments themselves.

In Russia in February 1917 there was very little sense of the difficulties that lay ahead. On 23 February bread queues formed in the capital. On 27 February the troops, the crucial element in maintaining order, joined in, refused to turn their weapons against the crowds, and that was the end of Tsarism. A Provisional Government was set up by members of the Duma or State Assembly, a government which stated that its brief was to rule Russia until a Constituent Assembly, elected on the base of universal suffrage, could decide the future form of government for the country. There was rejoicing in the major cities that the autocratic repressive system had ended. But conflicts very quickly revealed themselves, clashes of interests that were going to be very difficult to reconcile.

First there was disagreement over the continuation of the war, over the structure and organization of the army, and control of it. The Petrograd Soviet or Council of Workers and Soldiers' Deputies issued an Order Number 1 which abolished the existing draconian rules on discipline and sanctioned soldiers' committees. By such a move, it put on the agenda not only the question of the future structure, discipline, and authority within the army, but also the question of who within society should be the authority over the army: the Soviet, the Provisional Government, or the generals, now down in the south. A second issue, which increasingly came to the fore as the economy went into decline, involved the factories. Initially the conflicts were over wages, hours of work, and workers' rights but gradually they began to include the question of who should actually manage the factories. What should the rights of trade unions or factory committees *vis-à-vis* the managers or owners be, and to whom should the factories belong? Meanwhile, in the countryside the question of ownership was being settled by peasants simply taking the land, and village communities engaging in redistribution. We might suppose that this rural revolution in an 80 per cent peasant country should occupy pride of place in any account of what happened in 1917. But, while the peasant revolution was important for the indirect effect it had upon outcomes, and the peasant boys in army uniform played a direct part, it was developments within the major industrial centres, Petrograd and Moscow in particular, and within the army that mattered for the resolution of those key questions of authority and power.

In the big cities, during the period from February 1917 through until the autumn and after, a major social division revealed itself, one between the common people, the *narod*, or the lower classes, the *nizi*, comprising workers, peasants in army uniform, shop assistants, grave diggers, apprentices, and cab drivers on the one side and the upper classes, the *verkhi*, the privileged, on the other. Who were the privileged? They embraced professional people, members of the nobility, officers, civil servants, almost anyone who had an education. Popular hostility reflected itself in criticism, in jeering, in pushing and shoving those in a tram queue who wore spectacles. Spectacles went with education. 'All professors are bandits', a member of a search party remarked calmly to a professor whose flat he was searching. Wearing a winter coat or a jacket identified a member of the propertied classes. What characterizes that year is this division of urban society into two major blocks, in terms of what they saw their interests to be, their identification of the other. The issue of equality featured no less than those of food and work. 'Any talk of inequality is like a clip round the ear to a worker,' Zinoviev, a leading Bolshevik, remarked in 1921. The higher rations given to leading political officials were seen as 'privileges' and uneasily defended by their recipients; Lenin might advocate the paying of higher salaries to scarce specialists, but these could only be justified as 'temporary' and 'exceptions' to a proper order.

Whether the divide between the poor and the privileged can properly be called a class division, whether the ownership of property lay at its base, or was only one element within it, is a disputed question. As far as outcomes are concerned, however, the important point is that within those two blocks there was a splintering, a fragmentation that made cohesion extremely difficult. Among the poor, there were conflicts between skilled and unskilled workers, and between workers and soldiers over what they saw their interests to be. Among the privileged,

Tsarist officers and schoolteachers had little in common except being grouped together in the eyes of the poor. However, and this is important, there was greater cohesion in the demands, a greater ability to see themselves as sharing common interests on the part of the poor, and there was a language with which they could express their common interests—the language of socialism—and institutions (factory committees, soviets) which could and did press their case. The privileged never managed to get themselves together in the same way, to find a language through which they could express themselves, and institutions which could unite them.

What then were the demands being put forward by the poor and underprivileged? On the one hand there were those, not unique to the twentieth century, which tend to surface in situations in which a privileged and powerful élite is under attack. Such demands came to the fore at the time of the French Revolution and during the Chartist period in England, in Russia in 1917, during the Solidarity period in Poland, and they have appeared in Russia today: an end to privilege (equality comes high on the agenda), demands for their own representatives, for fair prices and wages, and for freedom from unjust laws. Such basic radical demands will, however, be accompanied by others, specific to the society and the time. By the time of the First World War key issues dominating European politics were those of the suffrage, national self-determination, and socialism. Already common currency among the small underground parties in Russia before 1917, they swept out into the open with the ending of Tsarism. Democracy was championed by almost all (and the demand for universal suffrage included votes for women); national self-determination became the banner of independence movements in different parts of the empire; socialism began to gain adherents as the summer wore on and the economic situation worsened. The end of Tsarism had not brought work and food, unemployment and lock-outs increased, and the Provisional Government stood by. In this environment the message of the socialist parties that ownership was the key, that only when the working people took over not merely land but factories could they achieve their demands, had a resonance. The more general aspirations of the poor found a particular framework, or strategy, on offer which suggested they could be realized. Increasingly the argument carried plausibility that only a workers' government could bring bread, justice, equality, and take society forward to that radiant kingdom the poor had always sought.

The Bolsheviks and the other more radical parties, the left wing of the Socialist Revolutionaries and the Anarchists, who advocated the working people taking power, and an end to the war, picked up support.

The Bolsheviks were one of two underground Marxist parties in Russia at the time of the First World War. In 1903 the original Russian Social Democratic Party had split over the question of tactics and organization into the Bolsheviks, led by Lenin, favouring a small, tightly knit party, able to avoid the Tsarist police, and the Mensheviks, in favour of a more broadly based, looser membership. In February the Bolshevik party was a party of just over twenty thousand, heavily working class but with intellectuals dominating its leadership. Its members had spent long periods in prison and working underground, working under false names in the factories where, ten or twenty years earlier as young apprentices, they had joined the party. Although the underground party never achieved the degree of organization and subordination to a central leadership that Lenin had advocated, its members, the undergrounders as they were subsequently called, had developed close ties one with another, and were used to the quarrelling, splitting, and heated disagreements that characterized underground party politics. After February this underground party became the core of the Bolshevik party, membership of which was now thrown open to all.

Both Bolsheviks and Mensheviks assumed, in February 1917, that Russia had now moved into a stage of capitalist development under a bourgeois government, a necessary stage of development before socialism could come on the agenda. When Lenin returned in April, however, he not only argued for an end to the war but also that it was already time to move forward to socialism. If Russia snapped the capitalist chain at its weakest link, in a world in which the advanced capitalist countries were ready for socialism, it could come to Russia too. By the force of his personality, and with support from some within the party, he swung the party round. A month later Trotsky, who had long been arguing for such a scenario, returned to Russia, and, with his entry into the party, added a powerful voice to the Bolshevik cause. Membership began to rise rapidly. The party was becoming one which included a small intellectual component, a solid core of metalworkers, highly skilled workers with long service in the factories, and now the young 17-year-olds with rifles over their shoulders, whether in the factories or in the army, these were recruits who six months before had never heard of the Bolsheviks, let alone of Marxism.

Let us consider the role played by political parties at this time. After the February revolution, political parties, now legalized, burst on to the scene: old parties, new parties, conservative, orthodox, liberal, socialist, anarchist. Eleven competed in Petrograd in the elections to the Constituent Assembly. Party membership rose and fell; some people joined several parties, which was surely more interesting than simply joining one. The parties were changing, fluid organizations to whom support was given and taken away. The emergence of a large number of parties, often small, many short lived, is a development that commonly accompanies the sudden ending of a dictatorial regime—we see it in Latin America, as military governments give way to civilian, in Algeria, in Eastern Europe (fifty-two parties in Hungary in 1990), and in the Soviet Union in 1990. An important question, to which we shall return, is whether this party proliferation is conducive to the establishment of a stable democratic order. Another, which concerns us here, is that of the role of parties in such a situation. They were very important in those summer months, channelling opinion, creating opinion, expressing it, producing ideas, raising the level of political discussion. It was a time of extraordinary political and social activity in a society previously deprived of opportunities to develop and express its views. A story is told of the chairman of a political meeting, at which the hall could not accommodate all who wished to attend, asking if those who had already had an opportunity to attend a *miting* (the English word passed into popular usage) would mind giving their places to those who never had. In such an environment, where settled patterns of existence are breaking up, political views can change very rapidly. People adopt positions quite unlike those of a year earlier, something which was very noticeable in the Soviet Union at the end of the 1980s. We need to ask ourselves whether, at such a time, voting for a party, or supporting a party, means the same thing as in parliamentary or liberal democracies, where there are established conventions on elections, on government, on the relationship between electorate, party, and legislature. No such conventions existed in Russia in 1917 or 1990.

By the late summer the deteriorating economic situation and the increasing polarization within society were cutting the ground away from under the political parties as institutions which could champion the different interests within society. The parties were yielding place to other political organizations, better able to express their constituents' demands: factory committees, trade unions, co-operatives, soldiers'

4001053

committees, the Red Guards, and, in Petrograd and Moscow, local soviets, local councils which were beginning to run local affairs, to patrol the streets, and to provide an element of welfare in a situation in which government had effectively broken down.

This brings us back to the Provisional Government and, more generally, to the question of political authority. Initially there was general acceptance from all except the monarchists that the Provisional Government was the, albeit temporary, rightful authority. Its composition changed over the months as members of the more moderate socialist parties, both Mensheviks and Socialist Revolutionaries, joined the remaining liberal Cadets, the Constitutional Democrats, in the government. However, this was a government which had little executive power. Its writ did not run throughout the country. It weakened itself by stressing that it was a caretaker government and that, therefore, it should not take major decisions on, for example, land reform; its ability to command the allegiance of the army was limited. Increasingly its authority was challenged by the soviets, those workers', soldiers', and peasants' councils which had first come into existence in 1905, then been suppressed, but whose memory had lived on and which re-emerged after February. The most important of these was the Petrograd Soviet. Dominated initially by Mensheviks and Socialist Revolutionaries its membership began to change during the summer, as factories and army regiments, in re-electing their delegates (a frequent practice in 1917), began to choose Bolsheviks. By July, frustrated by the failure of the Provisional Government to tackle the major issues, the sailors came down from Kronstadt, the naval base, and together with angry crowds surrounded the soviet, demanding that it take power. The soviet shrank from the task, the crowds were dispersed, and some of the leading Bolsheviks whose party had shown half-hearted support for the demonstration were arrested.

In this situation of deteriorating authority, force began to play an ever more visible role. It first found its expression in August in a march by General Kornilov, with troops loyal to him, on the capital. The aim was either to compel the Provisional Government, now led by Kerensky, member of a small Labour party, to take firm action as a government, or to establish a stronger, military form of rule. The attempt failed as Kerensky called upon the citizens to defend the revolution, arms were issued to factory workers (thus creating the future Red Guards), the troops turned out, and Kornilov's men refused to

fight. The threat from the right faded, but what the Kornilov attempt showed was that coercion was already stepping forward as the arbiter. There was still the hope, clung to by many, perhaps the majority, that elections to the Constituent Assembly would allow the issue of political authority to be resolved peaceably. But by September the situation was changing fast: the economic crisis was worsening, peasants were fast deserting the army to return home to claim land, and across the country, in some of the key cities, the soviets were gaining Bolshevik majorities. Their support was increasing too in sections of the army and on the battleships. At the major meetings being held in the capital, the Bolsheviks were picking up majority support.

We need though to be careful with our interpretation of actions at such a time. Let me give an example. An old lady, who at the time was a 17-year-old journalist beginning to identify with the Bolsheviks, told me of one of these meetings, held towards the end of September, and addressed by Trotsky. Trotsky was by then chairman of the Petrograd Soviet, a key figure in the Bolshevik party, and a brilliant speaker. At the meeting, attended by people of different political persuasions, he ended each section of his speech by asking the audience whether they supported the point he had made—on peace negotiations, on land, on workers' control—and in this way he built up to a climax where he had the whole meeting on its feet, cheering for the party, the Bolsheviks, that would realize these policies. She recounted how she had seen the Menshevik student leader from the Polytechnic Institute, shouting for the Bolsheviks together with everyone else, and, as they left the hall, she tapped him on the shoulder. 'So', she said, 'you have changed your position, have you? You are now one of us, a Bolshevik?' He shook his head as though to escape from a dream and replied, 'Give me a few hours to recover from Trotsky, and I'll be a Menshevik again.' Now, if political activists, members of political parties, could be swayed in one direction or another, we must recognize that the impact of political oratory (and it was a time of great oratory) on people without previous political experience could be considerable. We should see nothing strange in the same meeting changing its votes with different speakers. Support could be given one moment, taken away the next.

This raises the difficult question of what constitutes democratic action in such a situation. Lenin, at this time in hiding, was sending angry letters to the Bolshevik Central Committee, arguing that now was the time to act, now that the tide was sweeping in favour of radical demands; the party should make a bid for power while the opportunity was there. Not all members of the Central Committee were convinced: would they receive the necessary support and should it not be of the majority? Lenin's argument was that one should act in the interests of the majority, and thereby gain their subsequent support. Was that justified? He suggested that it was: the alternatives were either Kornilov and a military dictatorship or Bolshevik rule, hence it was criminal to wait. But Kamenev and Zinoviev, two members of the Central Committee, disagreed and published their disagreement in the press.

By October tension was rising in the capital. Delegates were beginning to arrive from all over the country for the Second Congress of Soviets (the first had been held in the summer); eyes were turning to the Bolsheviks, whose disagreements were public knowledge, but from whom some action was expected. People felt that something was going to happen. The action came from Kerensky, who sent troops to close down a Bolshevik printing press, and thus enabled Trotsky, chairman of a Military Revolutionary Council that had been set up by the Petrograd Soviet, to argue that the revolution was in danger. On 25 October the Council ordered loyal troops to take over key installations in the city, and to arrest the members of the Provisional Government. Its remaining members (Kerensky had managed to leave the city in a car borrowed from the American Embassy) sat in a corner room, high up in the Winter Palace, scribbling idly on their writing pads, unsure what action to take. Late at night, with a minimum of resistance, the Palace was taken by Bolshevik troops. Within a few days Kerensky returned, with troops loyal to the Provisional Government, and fighting took place on the outskirts of the city, but morale was low among Kerensky's supporters and the challenge faded away. Part of the problem was that, even before the Bolshevik seizure of power, support for the Provisional Government was ebbing away. The leaders of the Cadets, the strongest liberal party, had already reckoned that the time for electoral politics was over, and that force would be better employed in a cause other than that of saving the Provisional Government.

Meanwhile, at the opening of the Congress of Soviets, the Bolsheviks announced that power had passed to the soviets, and to a new government, the Council of People's Commissars, with Lenin as its chairman. The Left Socialist Revolutionaries, active in the Military Revolutionary Council, supported the Bolsheviks, and joined the government;

the Mensheviks and the Right Socialist Revolutionaries left the Congress in protest. Negotiations between the different socialist parties subsequently got under way, with the more moderate elements advocating a coalition socialist government of all parties, but excluding Lenin and Trotsky; the Bolsheviks themselves were divided but unenthusiastic, and the negotiations came to nothing. The new government sent troops to take over the old ministries, and attempted to ban (sometimes successfully, sometimes not) its opponents' newspapers. Street fighting in Moscow ended with a Bolshevik victory. Meanwhile elections to the Constituent Assembly were taking place across the country. The Bolsheviks won in Petrograd, in Moscow, and in some other major cities, but the results for the country as a whole produced an overwhelming victory for the Socialist Revolutionaries, the peasant party. Although the fact that the Socialist Revolutionaries had by this time split, with the Left supporting the seizure of power, makes the results less straightforward, it remains true that there was no way the Bolsheviks could claim a victory. By this time, however, they had abandoned any hope of electoral success; they had banned the Cadets, as counter-revolutionary, and were harrying their socialist opponents. When the Constituent Assembly met at the beginning of January, the Bolsheviks closed it, arguing that an Assembly which reflected backward peasant opinion could not dictate the future of the country. They possessed a higher authority, they claimed, which stemmed from their ability, as the party of the working class, to realize the interests of all the poor.

Let us return briefly to the interpretations outlined at the beginning of the chapter. Until the 1960s, the interpretation most popular among Western historians was the constitutional one, that which suggested Russia could have followed a path to liberal democracy had it not been for the Bolshevik seizure of power. But then historians began to question this, in large part because, in the 1950s and 1960s Third World countries, which had been provided with constitutions by the departing colonial powers, all too often abandoned a democratic path for one of military or one-party rule. This suggested that rural societies, plagued by poverty and underdevelopment, have particular problems in sustaining democratic rule. It became popular to argue that Russia could hardly have avoided some kind of authoritarian government. Soviet historians, meanwhile, clung to the standard class interpretation with its emphasis on class struggle, and a working class marching

forward under Bolshevik leadership. *Glasnost*, and then the undermining of the Communist Party's authority, opened the door to other
interpretations. Although a few stalwarts still support the traditional
view, among both historians and the wider public the constitutional
interpretation (economic progress under a democratic government was
a viable alternative to Bolshevism) and the cultural one (an enlightened
monarchist, religious regime was what Russia required) were the most
popular by the beginning of the 1990s. The reaction against the revolution itself was in full swing: placards demanded that Lenin, the name of
Satan, be taken away from St Peter's city; cities were renamed; quota-
tions culled from Lenin's works to show how he sent intellectuals to
their death were published; Tsarist ministers, Stolypin in particular
found a new popularity, fascination with the Tsarist family was reflected in the making of a film *The Last Days of the Tsar* (with a British
actor playing the Bolshevik responsible for the execution of the royal
family in 1918); and the heir to the throne was invited to visit St
Petersburg for the November 1991 celebrations. All this is indicative of
disillusionment, the feeling of being tricked about the country's history, and a reaction against a version too long unquestioned.

There are those who are tempted to argue that the Bolshevik regime
was little more than a throwback to an earlier more repressive stage in
Tsarist rule but, as of 1991, the suggestion that 1917 should not qualify
as a year of revolution was popular with neither Western nor Soviet
historians. Indeed it is difficult to see how, given the sweeping away of
the old propertied classes, and the emergence of a very different set of
rulers with a vision of a new society, it could be described as anything
else. The question, however, that was of far more interest in 1991 to
both Soviet historians and the wider public concerned what followed as
a *consequence* of the Bolshevik seizure of power. It is, therefore, to the
Bolsheviks as state-builders that we now turn.

TWO

State-Building: The Leninist System

WE suggested that a revolution is marked by violence, by the lack of central control over the means of coercion, and by freedom. During a revolution some individuals and institutions take matters into their own hands; others, on the contrary, feel helpless, at the mercy of forces they do not understand. It is a time when power lies scattered over the face of society, power drains away from the centre, down to the localities where a government writ no longer runs, where law and order break down, creating an environment for local initiatives and for crime. From this we can see that attempts to create a new basis of political authority, to re-establish political order, involve not merely the gaining of victory over opponents but also the ability to make laws and enforce them. Government, after all, involves deciding whose interests in society should be furthered and whose should be denied. State-building necessitates the curbing of freedoms, limiting autonomy, preventing actions, imposing order and constraints. All of this is inherent in the creation of political order out of a revolution. In that sense the process of state-building is anti-freedom, anti-autonomy, and anti-violence, although it may use violence in order to achieve the latter. The question is how, in the aftermath of a revolution, those imperatives inherent in the business of constructing a new political order are realized and concretized in a given situation. There is no guarantee that the new order will accord with the intentions of its creators; on the contrary, it is probably unlikely. The outcome will depend upon the interaction between the key actors, their aims and intentions, the options open to them, and the social context within which they are trying to realize them. Our concern is with that interaction in Soviet Russia between 1918 and 1921, and its results: the Leninist political system, whose key institutional features remained in place until 1989.

Very briefly, two words about the environment. First, it was one in which a civil war was waged between the Reds and the Whites, and with a third force, the Greens, a free-wheeling peasant army, operating in the countryside, in a country which had barely emerged from four years of fighting in the First World War. The fronts moved backwards and forwards across the territory, with the French and the British intervening when opportunities arose. The new political order was born out of a militarized environment, one in which social relationships had become brutalized, and the gun had become an accepted way of settling disputes. It was a time of atrocities on both sides, when old scores were settled and new conflicts arose. Second, the peasantry, the rural community, turned its back upon the towns. Peasant society withdrew, stepped back to an earlier stage of self-sufficiency, breaking its ties and the terms of trade with the urban centres. The Bolsheviks reacted with a policy of forced requisitioning in order to try to get grain out of the peasants for the towns. Meanwhile the White armies brought the landlords in their train, anxious to re-establish the old order. The peasantry either retreated still further, or defended itself with a force such as the Greens. Meanwhile the towns experienced economic decline, a slump as industrial resources failed and the railways seized up, and the haemorrhaging of population. Peasant workers streamed back to the countryside, industry slid to a halt, the towns became shadows of their former selves.

So much for the background. In January 1918 Russia's Bolshevik government had a precarious hold on power. The key question of who could establish military superiority remained to be resolved, the government's decrees were not accepted as binding, and its ability to employ sanctions to back up its questionable authority was very limited. What though were the aims of the Bolsheviks, the statebuilders, and how did they perceive their role? As we shall see, it was certain of their aims, in combination with the reality of fighting a war, that enabled them to lay the foundations of a political order. The framework, however, of this new state bore little resemblance to that either originally advocated by them or demanded on the streets of the cities.

First, what united the Bolsheviks? There was very little agreement within the party, whether leaders or rank and file, over most policy issues. They could not agree in the spring of 1918 whether to sign a peace treaty with Germany; they split over policy towards the peasants. On almost every issue, the Bolshevik leadership found itself divided. This was hardly surprising given that it found itself in a situation it had never prepared for, and faced with problems to which there were no obvious answers. Nor are we talking of a party with a tight organizational unity in which decisions taken by the leadership were effectively transmitted to or carried out by the rank and file. Certainly not in 1918. On the contrary it was a party with a fairly loose organization. Sverdlov, the undergrounder who took on the job of running the party's rudimentary Secretariat, kept most of the files in his head, with the consequence that when he died of influenza in 1919 they died with him. What, however, did unite the Bolshevik party? First, certain basic ideas. Second, and probably the most important, fighting a civil war forced the leaders to subsume their policy differences in order to concentrate on winning. Third, the very act of fighting a war created a new type of party, one which began to develop the organizational unity and internal discipline Lenin had suggested was necessary in Tsarist conditions and which subsequently, in Soviet mythology, was seen as an essential attribute of the party from its beginning.

The most basic idea, held in common by the Bolshevik leaders and the activists, was that they were the party of the working class, the vanguard class which was vital for constructing socialism, and which possessed a common interest. Only one party was therefore required to reflect that interest. Now, as 1918 progressed, as industry ground to a halt, and food shortages worsened, the already small working class began to shrink. Not only did the ex-peasants return home, but long-term workers joined the Red Army, or went out to help the revolution in the provinces. The standard of living dropped dramatically, and the government's popularity plummeted. By 1919, in Petrograd and Moscow, Bolshevik orators were being shouted down at factory meetings. So what should the Bolsheviks do? Did they consider backing out, that perhaps the revolution was premature, and the Mensheviks had been right to argue that Russia was too backward for socialism?

They never considered this option because they saw themselves as representing the working class in an era when socialism was on the agenda as an international fact. If in Russia the working class was disintegrating as a consequence of an imperialist war, and a civil war accompanied by foreign intervention, that in no way undermined their belief that socialism was waiting just round the corner in Europe and in America, and that they must keep the flame alight. They saw themselves as representing not merely the Russian working class but the international proletariat: that was their constituency. Telephone operators sat, expecting that any minute, any hour, the news would come through, from Berlin, from Paris, from London, that the revolution had happened there. Then the hours turned into days, and the days into weeks. Such a belief justified to the Bolsheviks their holding on, despite the protests, and it allowed them to argue that if an election did not return a Bolshevik majority, it could be ignored. We might well ask: why then continue with elections, if it had been decided that the backward strata in society should not determine the government? Why did the Bolsheviks continue with elections, in which they harried their socialist opponents and banned their publications? The reason was that they needed election results which reaffirmed their role as representing the workers' interests. They felt threatened by socialist opponents who, by their very existence, queried the Bolsheviks' right to speak for the class as a whole. We find them arguing that the aim should be a solid slate of Bolshevik deputies, then somehow party and working class would be a unity. The consequence was that the soviets, as democratic institutions reflecting all shades of working-class opinion, died. They became institutions which affirmed support for the government rather than bodies which either produced or controlled a government, and this remained their role until 1989.

A second belief, held in common by Bolsheviks, was that the government's task, and a relatively easy one once the representatives of the old order were defeated, was to realize society's common interest in its policies. In common with many others at the time, their image of the future society was that of a huge machine, a society running harmoniously according to a common purpose. Government was seen not as an operator, standing outside the machine, but rather as the oil which kept all the parts running smoothly, while the machine purred on. Machine and factory imagery was very popular in the first half of the century. One of the Bolshevik administrators, himself a metalworker by profession, wrote that 'the whole of society will be transformed into a single consumers-producers union, economic councils must make the whole people into the one powerful worker, spurred on by the general rule of common interests of the people. The whole country must turn into one huge factory.' The perception of society as made up of competing, conflicting interests, reflected in institutions, and in which the government advances some, denies others, and itself needs to be checked, was absent. And not surprisingly. For the Bolsheviks, as Marxists, the government performed that role in a class society, but with the end to private ownership the source of conflict dried up, and the clash of interests died. Until the old owners were finally defeated, the government's repressive functions would remain, but in the meantime it could act on behalf of the great majority, and thereafter gradually fade away. As a result, as state-builders the Bolsheviks made little attempt to delineate spheres of competence, to establish the rights of different government institutions *vis-à-vis* each other, or clarify the relations between central and local bodies.

They also believed that there was no need for a separate stratum of paid officials to administer policy. On the contrary it was important to involve as many as possible in the running of the country. Delegates would gather, take decisions, and return to their localities to implement them. Participatory democracy would be the hallmark of the new order. In line with this, we find that, as the soviets lost their decision-making functions, they retained elements that stemmed from this conception of government: they brought together people with little education and experience and those who had already moved up to administrative positions in the state apparatus, trade unions, or industry. In the early years they served as elementary schools for administrators who, it appeared, were necessary after all. Within such a framework, however, there was very little scope for control over the decision-makers who, increasingly, escaped from accountability, and established an executive chain of command operating downwards through the commissariats.

The final belief that had important consequences was that under a system of social ownership the workers' organizations would provide for, and indeed had an obligation to provide for, society's needs: be they food, work, health, education, or culture. The result was the emergence of an enormous number of institutions of all kinds. It proved impossible to provide the desired goods and services, but control by the state over their *distribution* was seen as a way of realizing the aim of equality. Some of them were the result of local initiative, of people taking things into their own hands—setting up courts, a militia, organizing house committees or co-operatives—trying desperately to distribute the scarce resources. But the resources shrank, and to the Bolsheviks' dismay the number of bureaucratic institutions grew. The new government ministries, the commissariats, employed more and more staff as they attempted to organize and administer the economy and services. By 1921 Lenin was talking of the antheap of bureaucracy that existed in Moscow, the new seat of the government. Offices multiplied, paperwork piled up, while the queues lengthened outside. The situation was exacerbated by the collapse of industry and trade, as people, desperate for a ration card, moved into government offices. Rivalry developed between the institutions, whose powers were ill-defined, and bureaucratic practices increased.

The new rulers, the Bolsheviks, still a small party of political activists, resorted to different strategies to try to run this burgeoning state. First they placed Bolsheviks in charge of new and old institutions—whether army regiments, factories, hospitals, universities or food supply depots—in order to try to ensure that they operated properly. Putting loyal party activists in charge of key institutions quickly became standard practice, and subsequently grew into the extensive *nomenklatura* system, under which party bodies became responsible for the promotion and appointment of leading personnel in all society's institutions. This was accompanied by the conviction that the social background of the personnel determines whether an institution functions well or badly, rather than its structure or relationship to other institutions. Second, the Bolshevik party came to be seen as the mechanic who would adjust and control this machine whose parts were not working in unison. A war, after all, needed to be won, and direction and control were vital. Increasingly the Bolshevik party resorted to giving orders and instructions which were obligatory for the state apparatus.

Frustrated by the inefficiency of the new institutions, and desperate to maintain the war effort, the Bolshevik leadership strove to establish for itself a position over and above the state organizations, a position from which it, unrestrained, could take decisions which would cut through the bureaucratic tangles. An unaccountable leadership emerged, relying ever more on a militarized Bolshevik party which received its orders from above, and whose membership was becoming concentrated in the army and the police. Military methods spread over into civilian organizations, boundaries between the two became blurred. In December 1917 the government had set up a new organization, the Cheka, responsible to it, whose brief was to combat banditry, i.e. large-scale armed robbery, and to uncover speculation and

sabotage. It was to lay bare those activities associated in Bolshevik minds with the old order, with buying and selling scarce resources for a profit, and also to root out counter-revolution, whether in printed form, demonstrations, or plots against the government. We see here a blurring of the boundaries between the political and the criminal, and one organization with responsibilities for both. As the civil war continued, any action which ran counter to government policy became identified as counter-revolutionary: speculation, an opposition printing press, or a strike for higher rations. Given the argument that Bolshevik power was representing the interests of the great majority, any actions against the government were characterized as anti-social, and hence counter-revolutionary.

By the autumn of 1920 the Red Army had won the civil war, and Russia had a Bolshevik government in military control of the country, and with a centralized government structure able to carry out policies. There was, however, grave disquiet on the part of the leadership over the political and social order that had emerged. On the one hand there was the state bureaucracy, on the other industrial ruin stared the country in the face. And it was industry that had been seen as the prerequisite for socialism: essential for the provision of the goods and services in order that all could live a decent life. The aim had been a highly productive, industrial sector, manned and run by conscious, educated, skilled workers. Instead there was a devastated industry, lacking both the economic resources and a class-conscious proletariat capable of running the country. So what was to be done? The party found itself locked in bitter debate. Should it impose discipline in the name of the working class, simply impose order, dictatorially, militarize the economy and drive it forward, or should it democratize both industry and the party (was it the new élitist practices that were partly to blame?) and reckon on the class-consciousness of the remaining workers? This was the debate that preoccupied the party during the winter months of 1920 and early 1921, a debate which threatened to split it apart.

As the party argued, in the spring of 1921, peasant revolts against the force td requisitioning of grain began to spread, workers in Petrograd came out on strike, and the Kronstadt soldiers mutinied, demanding free trade and a return to soviet democracy. The party closed its ranks and suppressed the revolts. It did that without question. Part of the inhe eritance of the civil war was the conviction that any actions which either challenged the Bolshevik government's right to rule *or its policies* must be suppressed. Political opposition would have no place in the future political order. This was the last challenge, the last flicker of opposition to Bolshevik rule; hereafter the political authority of the party remained unchallenged. It had defeated its opponents, established a working mechanism of government, and could call upon sufficient support from within the urban sector to maintain it. It was still only recognized as the rightful government by a minority of the population but over time this would change.

In 1921 it badly needed a strategy to cope with the problems facing it. As far as the economy was concerned, the leadership, albeit reluctantly, resorted to old methods to revive industry. Even during the civil war, faced with the catastrophic fall in productivity, piece-work had been introduced, and Lenin had argued consistently for the employment of the bourgeois specialists at higher salaries. Together with one-man management, these became part of the post-war factory. Equality was to be forgone for the time being. As part of a New Economic Policy, announced in March 1921, small-scale industry returned to private ownership, free trade was authorized, forced requisitioning ended, and the renting out of land and hiring of some labour by the peasantry was allowed. Russia, it was argued, was too poor and too backward to introduce immediately those socialist relationships of production that had been hoped for in 1917. How then were these old, exploitative, ways of producing and distributing society's goods to be prevented from imposing their values upon society? How were they to counter a slipping back to the old unjust order? The Bolshevik answer lay in putting politics in command. If the economy was too backward and the desired class-consciousness was not there, then political action would be needed to refashion the economic base and the educational sphere. The new state apparatus, however, also reflected society's backwardness; its bureaucratic practices were witness to that. The machine needed an operator and that meant the party, a party pruned of its undesirable elements, armed with its knowledge of Marxism, and committed to the interests of the working class. If the working class was too weak, the party must act for it. Its task was to transform society and then, and only then, would politics and the state wither away. In such an order of things, the soviets and the trade unions had a role as educational institutions but they should not, they could not be allowed to, act independently of the party, the political leader.

How though had the civil war affected the Bolshevik party? It had become very much a two-layered party. On the one hand there were the undergrounders, those with pre-revolutionary experience, who had made a conscious choice to join a socialist party. That did not mean they agreed with one another over policies, but they shared a common past, something quite lacking in the new recruits. By now the stratum of old undergrounders was very thin indeed, no more than 3 per cent of the membership. They had taken a hammering out on the battlefields, or from working twenty-four hours a day as the new administrators. Many were sick, worn out. But it was this group who occupied the leadership positions in the new state institutions and in the party itself. Then there were the recent recruits. By 1920 the Nineteen-Seven-teeners, the young factory workers who had come into the party in 1917, were considered old hands compared with the Nineteen-Nineteeners, the peasant boys brought in through the Red Army, and the new re-cruits in the towns. Skilled workers hardly existed any longer, so the party had recruited women—those unreliable comrades in arms—barbers, apprentices, and policemen. They were a far cry from the class-conscious proletariat that the underground party used to look to as its natural recruiting ground. They were politically ignorant. By 1921 it was reckoned that less than a quarter of the party had ever read Marx. They were poorly educated, they drank too much, a few still went to church. And this was meant to be the proletarian party that would lead society forward. What then should the policy of the leadership towards its own party be? Should it throw out all those politically unreliable, untested members and concentrate on being a small politically pure party, or should it continue to bring in those whose only qualification was that they should be able to read and write, and then educate them? That would be one way of identifying the party with the rank and file in the factories, in the offices, and out in the fields.

The question of the party's relationship to the working class or to the wider public was never, in the whole of the period from 1921 through to 1991, properly resolved. The line swung one way and then another. At one time the emphasis was on purging the unreliable elements, restric-ting the ranks in the belief that only then could the party play a van-guard role, leading, providing an example for the rest of society. Then the other strategy would come into play: opening the party's ranks to working-class recruits of all kinds in an attempt to keep the party a party with its roots in the factory floor. The first membership purge occurred in 1921 as the leadership sought to weed out unreliable elements; by the mid-1920s the recruitment drive was in full swing again. The point that concerns us here, however, is that, by the end of 1920, the existence of a politically ignorant rank and file encouraged the old undergrounders to issue orders, and to treat the recruits like private soldiers in an army, thus producing tension within the organization as older democratic practices rubbed up against those of an élitist, militarized body. It was not going to be easy, it was recognized, for the party to retain its purity in the dangerous environment of the New Economic Policy, in which elements of capitalism were being reintroduced, and there was the added problem of a fractious party, split and squabbling. At the Xth Party Congress, in March 1921, as delegates returned from suppressing the Kronstadt revolt, and the New Economic Policy was agreed, Lenin proposed a ban on factions within the party. After debate and against some opposition, but with most reluctantly agreeing that unity was vital for the party's survival, the Congress resolved to ban the organizing of factions.

We can now put together the key elements in the Leninist political framework which provided the basis for a new state. The party whose authority, it was claimed, stemmed from its ability to take society forward to a society of justice, equality, and plenty, was seen as the moral guarantor of the political system: it controlled the means of coercion, the greater part of the means of communication, and some of the economic resources; it was responsible for policy and appointments. The soviets, trade unions, and other mass organizations would help to administer policy and to educate society under the guidance of the party, which would oversee the state apparatus but would not interfere with its work. Political opposition was ruled out. Are there not, however, serious problems with this as a structure of government, quite regardless of whether one approves of the moral and political assumptions upon which it rests? First, it is difficult to see how the party was to lead and control but not to interfere in government administration, if things were not working well. Second, and more important, what was the guarantee that the party would manage to retain its political purity and, third, how was it to identify and agree on what the interests of society were? All were to surface, with drastic consequences, in the years that followed.

THREE

Industrialization, Collectivization, and the Stalinist State

THE question whether traditional Russian society or the revolution, whether backwardness, the Bolshevik party, or indeed Stalin himself, were the cause of, or contributed to, the Stalinist dictatorship is one of endless debate. We cannot do it justice here. Our aim is more modest: to show how some features of the Leninist system, and some actions taken by the leading Bolsheviks, worked together to produce a powerful, centralized state, but one with built-in conflict and instability. We approach the subject by looking, first, at the problems posed for the Bolshevik leadership by Lenin's death and the need to find a way forward for a backward country seeking industrialization; second, at the industrialization and collectivization campaigns that followed; and, third, at the accompanying political developments which resulted in the Stalinist system of the mid-1930s, as it existed before the onset of the Great Purge.

In December 1922 Lenin had a stroke from which he never fully recovered and in January 1924 he died. With his death, a joint leadership, known as the triumvirate, was formed from Kamenev, Zinoviev, and Stalin. Stalin held the, as yet, less important post of Secretary of the party. Siding with them was Bukharin, the youngest of the party leaders, the 'darling of the party', the ablest theoretician among them. The individual upon whom all eyes were focused, however, was Trotsky, the potential Bonaparte of the revolution. At the time of the revolution and afterwards the Bolsheviks continually looked back over their shoulders to the French Revolution. They discussed it endlessly. Did revolutions follow the same path? Would the Russian revolution devour its own children, would a Bonaparte arise and take over? If there was to be a Bonaparte, it was clear it would be Trotsky, the flamboyant orator, leader of the Red Army, and advocate of military discipline in the economy. When Lenin died, he left a short written piece, subsequently known as his testament, which was distributed at a Party Congress and caused embarrassment to all. Here was Lenin, in his last words to the party, writing of the character failings of the individual Bolshevik leaders he left behind. What did he say? He reminded his colleagues that Kamenev and Zinoviev wavered in October 1917 over whether the time was right for revolution. He criticized Bukharin for sometimes lacking political judgement, despite his theoretical ability; and, after praising Trotsky's political and organizational abilities, he reminded all that Trotsky was a latecomer to Bolshevism. Of Stalin he wrote, 'Stalin has amassed great power into his hands as Secretary and I am not sure whether he will always use it wisely'; he referred to Stalin's rudeness, his lack of tact, and raised the question of removing him from the post of Secretary. The testament was welcome news to none and, after a brief discussion, his heirs decided to put it away and get on with the business of ruling. Although its contents were widely known in the party at the time, its existence was subsequently forgotten and when, in 1956, Khrushchev referred to it, it was a revelation to all but a few.

Here, however, a different question concerns us. Was it not odd for Lenin to write of individual characteristics and not of the class nature of society in his last message to his colleagues? There was, however, a good reason for his doing so. The very difficult economic situation, towards which the party had no agreed policy, was necessarily going to result in intense debate and conflict within a group of extraordinarily able and different individuals. There was still a danger of the party splitting. It was therefore one of those historical situations in which personality and the individual were going to play their part in determining outcomes. Lenin's heirs were well aware of this, and it made them nervous.

In the circumstances they adopted two policies which were disastrous for the future. First, they tried and succeeded in restricting debate as far as possible to a small circle. They did not throw the debates, and their resolution, open to the party as a whole. In their anxiety over factions splitting the party, and their lack of confidence in the political expertise of the membership as a whole, they resorted to settling the conflicts that arose among themselves. This meant that when Trotsky and what became known as the Left Opposition found themselves, in 1925, failing to get a proper hearing at party meetings, it was extremely difficult for them to argue for greater democracy within the party and to accuse their opponents of being undemocratic, when they themselves had been in favour of restricted debate. This, as we shall see, had serious consequences for relationships within the party.

The second tactic, employed by the leadership, was to create a cult of Lenin. Lenin became that symbol of unity so desperately needed to mask the disunity that existed at the top of the party. Without Lenin's authority to override the conflicts, the party was in trouble, and so his successors paid homage and tried to bind the party together by invoking its now mystical leader. They needed a symbolic authority to which they could appeal, and which could be presented to the party. A Lenin cult emerged with poems, pictures, oaths, and incantations: 'Lenin lives in the soul of every member of our party, every member of our party is a particle of Lenin. Our entire Communist family is a collective embodiment of Lenin.' A competition was announced for the best memorial to him. One entry which did not win but which captured the mood of the times was for Lenin's embalmed body to lie at the base of a huge glass telephone exchange in Red Square. All who passed by would look up, from their shopping, and see the telephone operators in that wonderful monument to modern technology, linking Red Square with New York, Berlin, or Delhi, while Lenin slept below. It was too expensive, alas. Lenin's embalmed body was placed in a modest mausoleum, where, from 1953 to 1961, it was joined by that of Stalin, and became a place of pilgrimage for millions of Soviet and foreign citizens. In 1991 discussion centred on whether Lenin had asked to be buried beside his mother in St Petersburg and, if so, whether the request should be honoured; or whether, perhaps, foreign currency could be earned by sending his embalmed body on an overseas tour.

In the mid-1920s too foreign currency would have been very welcome. The debate over the way forward was important not just for its outcome for Russia but also because it brings before us a key problem of the twentieth century. The Bolshevik leadership was struggling, as one of them put it, to find an answer to the problem of how a poverty-stricken country could scrape together the capital required for industrialization. This was a question that has increasingly preoccupied leaders in the Third World as the twentieth century has unfolded: how could their countries make that leap into industrialization that Western Europe and North America had made a century earlier? As we might expect, given the intellectual calibre of individuals such as Bukharin and Trotsky, the debate brought out the issues in all their sharpness.

The New Economic Policy, the NEP, was intended to get the shattered economy on its feet again with a mixture of state ownership, private ownership, and private agriculture, and to rebuild the terms of trade between town and country. In 1921 all had agreed, reluctantly, that these measures were necessary. By 1923, however, Trotsky and the Left Opposition were arguing for a policy shift. The leading economist among them, Preobrazhensky, argued as follows. The already poor Russian economy had been thrown off balance first by the First World War and then by the civil war. On the one hand, with the destruction of plant and machinery, the capital stock had shrunk and, on the other, with the break-up of the estates into small family farms, peasants were eating more: consumption had risen relative to savings. Demand for industrial goods of all kinds was high, but industry was quite incapable of producing them. If industry could not produce goods to sell to the peasants, it would not receive grain and agricultural products in return. Therefore, Preobrazhensky argued, all efforts must be concentrated on expanding the capital goods sector. Unless the country had an industrial base capable of producing the machinery which could then spin cloth, the plants which could turn out the bicycles, the radios, oil lamps, and agricultural implements the peasants wanted, the towns would never get the produce from the countryside that was needed to feed the urban population, and the raw materials for industry and for export. Investment for heavy industry was the key. Where, however, was it to come from? Industry was too small and too poor to be able to provide sufficient real savings. The government could and should turn to the urban workers to ask them to tighten their belts and forgo wage increases; it could sell state bonds, and try to make industrial production more efficient, but there was no way these measures could provide the necessary capital.

How had the capitalist economies done it? They had plundered agriculture, exploited their own working class, and the imperialist powers had extracted resources from their colonies but, as a socialist state, Preobrazhensky argued, such avenues were closed to Soviet Russia. Somehow though the investment had to be found: the only way, he suggested, was to tax the peasants. As he put it: 'A country like the USSR with its ruined and in general rather backward economy must pass through a period of primitive socialist accumulation in which the forces provided by the pre-socialist forms of the economy [i.e. private agriculture] must be drawn upon very freely'. In other words, resources had to be extracted from the peasants; a policy of squeezing the peasantry should be combined with the introduction, gradually and on a small scale, of collectivization or social ownership in agriculture because, it was argued, large-scale socially owned farms would be more efficient than small-scale private farming.

These proposals which were effectively calling for an end to NEP failed to make headway during 1923–7. The dominant view at the time, associated with Bukharin and still advocated by him and what became known as the Right Opposition after 1928 when the policy shifted, disputed the Left's policy prescriptions. Bukharin's argument ran as follows. Of course it was true that industry needed investment, but the economy as a whole needed investment, not just industry, but agriculture too. The Left Opposition's suggestion that the country would achieve maximum industrial growth rates if large transfers were made from the agricultural to the industrial sector was, Bukharin argued, simply incorrect. Only if agriculture expanded, only with a productive agriculture would the resources be there that could sustain meaningful transfers from the agricultural sector. In other words, industry could only grow if agriculture grew first or, at the very least, simultaneously. Then agriculture would be able to produce food for the towns and raw materials for industry and for export which would allow the import of the heavy industrial equipment that was needed. If, Bukharin argued, if they squeezed the peasantry now, they would kill the goose that laid the golden eggs. It was too early to think of extracting resources from the peasantry by taxing them. On the contrary, what was needed was a pro-peasant policy. He spoke of riding into socialism on a peasant nag and, in a famous phrase, called upon the peasants 'to enrich themselves'. The Left's recommendations, he argued, would only damage the economy; the way forward to socialism had to be a gradual one.

It is instructive to try to decide which of the arguments are the more convincing; to ask which economic and political considerations, either at the time or from the perspective of today, would persuade one to defend the Left or the Right position. Both were fraught with danger.

As of today it is unclear that there is *any* 'solution' to the problem of backwardness that does not bring untold suffering to sections of the population. On what basis, then, should decisions be made? In 1925 Kamenev and Zinoviev began to distance themselves from Stalin, and to query the continuation of the NEP on the same terms. By 1926 they were seeking an alliance with the defeated Trotsky, but it was too late. Stalin and Bukharin outmanœuvred them in the central party bodies. The pro-peasant policy held until 1927 by which time pre-war levels of industrial production had been regained. The economy was in better shape but productivity was low, unemployment high, and growth still slow. The problem of moving from a rural to an industrialized economy was no nearer solution. This was the context in which, at the Party Congress in 1927, a decision was taken that industrialization should be put firmly on the agenda with a new five-year plan, in which there would be a much greater emphasis on expanding the industrial sector. Although the intent was clearly stated, an element of wishful thinking still prevailed as far as the resources for investment were concerned, but once industrial development began in earnest, in 1928, the question could no longer be avoided.

It was at that point that Stalin, arguing that the *kulaks*, the wealthy peasants, were holding the towns to ransom by not marketing their grain until the price should rise, sent out an expeditionary force to extract grain at gun point. Censured by the Politburo for using force, he returned to the attack with a policy recommendation for collectivization. His argument was as follows. If the government expropriated the *kulaks*, who exploited the poorer peasants and held back their grain, and introduced large state or co-operative farms with the back-up of tractors and new technology, the result would be a more productive agriculture which would not only produce food for the towns, and grain for export, but also a higher standard of living for the peasants. It was his advocacy of this that produced the Right Opposition, opposed to such drastic measures in agriculture. Now, however, it was Bukharin's turn to find himself in a minority, and Stalin emerged as undisputed leader.

From 1928 to 1932 Russia, and the other Soviet republics, experienced a 'Revolution from Above', as it was called, in which the political leadership established a system of state ownership of the means of production and a centrally planned economy. Very briefly we will describe the campaigns that created this new 'socialist' base. The first five-year plan called for higher investment and output in the heavy industry sector: mining, iron and steel, energy, lathes, and tractors. But very quickly the original targets were scrapped and replaced by higher ones: construction fever, competition, pressures towards fulfilling and overfulfilling the plan swept the country. The size of the industrial labour force more than doubled; conditions deteriorated; labour turn-over rocketed as construction workers and peasants moved from job to job in search of food and housing. Barrack towns arose in the steppes; peasants slept in manholes in the cities; hordes of orphaned children lived in gangs in the pipes on the construction sites, vanishing like rats when daylight broke. Resources—raw materials and labour—were thrown, without thought, into the great endeavour which, by 1932, was claimed to have succeeded: the Soviet Union had laid down a heavy industrial basis, the pre-condition for both armaments and a consumer-goods industry. In fact, however, only some of the plan's targets had been reached and at the cost of using and tying up, in unfinished projects, a huge amount of resources. Of more concern to us is the way the centrally planned economy was run, what planning meant in practice.

It is easy to imagine a plan in which all the outputs would be specified, and dovetailed with all the inputs required, a neat and exact plan in which all would be accounted for ahead of time, and then executed. In the Soviet context, nothing like this ever existed, even in imagination. The PLAN meant something rather different, i.e. the identification of targets for priority sectors (in heavy industry) or prod-ucts, and the earmarking of resources for them; the setting of targets for light industry, and specifiying the inputs, but these might or might not be available; and setting delivery targets for the collective and state farms. All efforts were concentrated, not merely on fulfilling the plans for industrial output but on overfulfilling them. Now that immediately tells us that the framework was not one of a beautiful planned economy because, had it been such, overfulfilling would cause havoc.

From the early 1930s onwards, the Soviet Union had a three-sector economy: heavy industry and defence as the priority sector, light indus-try a poor second, and then agriculture. Under Stalin it was a law of socialism that heavy industry should grow at a faster rate than light. Heavy industry got the resources, the skilled labour, the privileges, the status. The economy was administered through a series of what we would call nationalized industries, run from Moscow by ministries, each responsible for a different branch of industry, and issuing plans and instructions to the enterprises below. It was then a hierarchical system, with commands being issued from the centre to the producing units. This was subsequently, post-1985, rightly referred to as the Administrative-Command System, a system under which the economy was run from above through the medium of a central plan, targets, and administrative orders. However, simultaneously, implicit in the conception was a notion of enthusiasm and participation from below: the work-force would not simply carry out the commands from above, rather they would strive to fulfil them and overfulfil them. In the chaotic early 1930s, and again in the post-war period as hundreds of thousands threw themselves into making good the devastation wrought by the German invasion, this curious combination of target-planning and appeals to a social patriotism gave the economy a momentum. But the ministerial and planning-from-above system led to the development of large bureaucratic structures, jealously guarding an individual industry's interests, i.e. its share of resources, and, with no need to search for profitability, substituting the elaboration of administrative controls and detailed instructions for innovation and incentives. The more ministerial control, the less room for initiative or participation.

If central administrative control was one aspect of the system, campaigns were the other. It was a time of campaigns, campaignology, as one Western writer has described it. The centre would initiate a policy, issue commands, and mobilize the troops, but, unlike a military manœuvre, the campaigns sometimes acquired a momentum of their own and ran out of control. Collectivization was just such a one. Stalin's arguments surely persuaded some, others were probably inspired by the desire to pull Russia for ever out of peasant backwardness, others were fearful of the consequences, but whatever the hopes and motivations, the result was a civil war in the countryside. Out went sections of the Red Army, and in came the troops of the Commissariat of Internal Affair, the NKVD, young Komsomol activists, industrial workers, and students, to carry the campaign to the countryside. When Lenin died in 1924 the party's doors were flung open to a mass enrolment. In some instances whole factories enrolled in the party. New members tended to be young urban workers, apprentices maybe, those who had been children at the time of the revolution and were impatient to proceed with the business of building socialism.

They were an interesting generation, in their black leather jackets,

with their macho image, often puritanical, anti-smoking, anti-drinking, and anti-dancing (campaigning against 'foxtrotism', the most popular dance of the twenties). Their attitude to sex varied, being both puritanical and matter of fact. Marriage was out, very bourgeois, freedom all important. Self-improvement, a social commitment, intolerance of anything associated with the old order were all characteristics of this generation. A League of Time, whose members kept diaries in which they noted each moment's activities in order not to waste any time, attracted thousands. Time-keeping became an obsession, probably partly linked with the change from a peasant to an industrial economy in which time is measured differently. These recruits to the party and the Komsomol, the youth organization, were very critical of the old bourgeois specialists, the pre-revolutionary professors, critical even of party intellectuals and undergrounders who advocated caution. They wanted to see an end to youth unemployment, to the NEP men, to peasant ignorance, to Russia's backwardness, and they were prepared to act as the shock troops of industrialization and collectivization. And not only out on the construction sites or in the countryside. They were anxious to see a five-year plan for the Arts, to call the bourgeois professors to order, and to eradicate religion wherever possible.

Out in the countryside rich peasants were rounded up, packed into trucks, and deported to Siberia, if they were not shot on the spot. For the first time in Russian history, peasants died of overeating as they killed and ate their own livestock rather than lose them to a collective farm. Millions died. In the spring of 1930, with chaos in the countryside and no sowing taking place, Stalin called a temporary halt. Then the campaign was renewed, producing famine in parts of the countryside. By 1933 the central authorities had gained control of agriculture in the sense of having broken peasant resistance and replaced private farms with a system of collective farms and state farms. Several villages might constitute one farm; the peasants lived, as before, in their private houses and had small plots of land on which to grow produce, rear chickens, a pig or possibly a cow, but all the farmland was now held collectively, and a farm manager was responsible for seeing that the collective farm produced the quota set for it by the regional authorities. The peasants were obliged to work for the collective farm, and only got 'paid' from a surplus left after the quota had been delivered. Many of them lived off their private plots; some sold the produce in the local town market, at free prices, if there was a town in the vicinity. Although output began to rise again in the late 1930s, and the towns were fed, agriculture remained an impoverished sector. The tractors which did appear never made up for the lost livestock; the young men, and women, left in their millions, either recruited or voluntarily, for the construction sites and the towns.

This was the quicksand society, as one historian has described it, characterized by a population on the move, restless and bewildered, and by enormous social mobility. Industrialization and collectivization, set in motion by the authorities, resulted in a society in flux over which the government found itself struggling unsuccessfully to impose its will. The search for bourgeois saboteurs, when things went wrong in industry, was taken up with alacrity by a younger generation; artists, professors, and writers found themselves called to account by impatient and intolerant Komsomol activists. The old Bolsheviks still retained the leading positions in the ever-expanding party-state apparatus, although Trotsky was in exile abroad, and Kamenev, Zinoviev, and Bukharin on the sidelines, but they were being joined by a new energetic, utterly committed, group, many of whom had come from poor backgrounds, acquired a basic education, and moved to positions of responsibility. Nikita Khrushchev, a peasant boy from the mines, was just such a one; by the mid-1930s he was shouting orders, cursing, and encouraging, as he struggled through the water and the mud of that future showpiece of socialism, the Moscow Metro. For the Khrushchev generation, the period of the first five-year plan remained the heroic period of their lives, the one which laid the basis for socialism and established the Soviet Union as a society of a new kind, far superior to the decadent and dying capitalist countries of the West, then in the grip of the Great Depression. This was a time when people emigrated from the West to the Soviet Union, in search of work and to participate in the building of a new society. The havoc and suffering in the countryside, while recognized by the young Khrushchevs, was justified in terms of the future they were building, and subsequently forgotten in the history books. Children were being born whose proud parents named them Little-Five-Years or Revolution, if a girl, Plan or Vil (from Lenin's initials), if a boy. Mikhail Gorbachev was born at this time, down in the rural south.

Meanwhile the ruling authorities were trying desperately to regain control of this moving, shapeless society by giving those who occupied the leading positions in the administrative structures power and privileges, by introducing sharper income differentials, and by employing coercion. By the mid-1930s, the political authorities, the rulers, had taken over the economy, the media, and all social activities. The state apparatus that emerged consisted of centralized hierarchical institutions, both industrial and other ministries operating from the centre, sending instructions down, and competing with each other for resources. One among them, the NKVD, the Commissariat of Internal Affairs, had gained in importance as the leadership resorted to using coercion against the peasants, to trials of bourgeois specialists, and to rooting out opposition and criticism inside the party. What, however, held these institutions, responsible for the economy, for culture, and for law and order, together? How were disputes between them resolved, how was coercion held in check? It was the party which was meant to bind them together by providing leadership from above and, through its network of full-time party officials, the party apparatus, to transmit orders from the centre to all the relevant institutions, and to check the working of the ever-growing state apparatus. Meanwhile it was for the committed membership, carrying out orders, and setting an example for their fellow workers in factories and institutions, to inspire and educate the population in its civic duty.

For the party to be able to do this, it would need to have a leadership in agreement on policy and, second, an organization whose members were working together. In 1934 Stalin argued that the party was united as it had never been before. Given its past history that was perhaps not a difficult claim to make, but what kind of unity was this, and how had it been achieved? This brings us back to the question of how the Leninist arrangements—a vanguard party leading and overseeing a state apparatus—could work in practice, and what the political consequences of industrialization and collectivization were for party and state. We begin with the party. Another wave of recruitment had accompanied the industrialization and collectivization campaigns. The ranks of the party were swollen not only with hundreds and thousands of young workers and peasants, but also with those, of different backgrounds, who made up the new managerial and government élite. Again the leadership drew back, called for a review of party cards, and in 1933 expelled nearly 20 per cent of the membership for corruption, careerism, alcoholism, and other unworthy behaviour. There was nothing very new here. But by now the party officials, the core of the new élite, whether at central or regional level, were powerful individuals indeed. These were the individuals who moved up the party hierarchy, from factory, to district, to regional, and then possibly to the central party apparatus. There were others, meanwhile, who specialized in ideological work, in the army, in the media, or in industry. They were responsible for overseeing the economy, production and distribution, for the maintenance of order, and for education and culture. All major resources were gathered into their hands. They appointed the state officials; they were answerable to the centre for results. We find them bossing, domineering, issuing orders, trying to control and manage all around them. But was this Lenin's vanguard party, leading, but not interfering, as the soviet state structures developed into those of self-administration? Hardly. But what was at fault was the concept of a vanguard party, pure and knowledgeable, able to stand apart and yet be in charge. There was no way it could do this. Inevitably its officials, responsible for the use of resources, involved themselves in their management, identified with the sectors they were answerable for, and became part of a party–state apparatus. Regional officials identified with regional interests; others with a particular industry or sphere of government. The central party leadership responded by shifting its officials around, stressing the 'generalist' qualities of its lieutenants, and it did succeed in fashioning a body of men (and they were largely men) who saw themselves as administrators, managers, in whatever sphere the party called them to. But while it was an élite with an *esprit de corps*, its members, by virtue of being responsible for running all society's activities, repeatedly found themselves sucked into the institutional structures that cast an administrative web over the whole. The Leninist arrangements became more and more difficult to maintain as the political realm made itself directly responsible for managing all society's resources, and drew into itself all the conflicts of interests. The concentration of power may have unforeseen consequences: its holders may find themselves less able to control, let alone transform, society; commands can be an ineffective way of ruling; there may be more conflict, albeit of a different kind, than in a society where power is shared.

The leadership responded by emphasizing more and more strongly the need for democratic centralism, for the carrying out of orders from above without criticism, without discussion. If the party could not generate unity of action from within, it must be imposed from above. The emphasis on using discipline to create the required organizational unity was accompanied by the assertion that if policies were not carried out successfully the fault must lie with the individuals concerned. All could be solved by putting the right people in the right place. Organization and personnel were what mattered.

An image which Stalin subsequently employed was that of the party as an orchestra and, for him, unlike those musicians who after the revolution had argued that in the new socialist society orchestras would play in harmony without a conductor, the role of conductor was vital. This brings us to the question of leadership. In both the Soviet Union and other Communist Party regimes we notice a tendency not merely for a single leader to emerge (despite attempts at collective leadership) but for a severe *personalization* of leadership, including the creation of a cult around the leader. (This only happened retrospectively with Lenin, which is something very different.) Stalin, Mao, Ceauçescu, Kim Il Sung, even the ageing Honecker and Brezhnev, with more or less success, enjoyed a cult. The phenomenon cannot then be explained in terms of a country's tradition or culture since it occurred in societies without any such tradition. Its roots, we suggest, lie in the concept and practice of the vanguard party. The party's right to rule, it was claimed, lay in its ability to find the best, true, way forward for society. As we saw, however, its leaders disagreed on what this was, thereby threatening the party's very basis of authority, and, as they sought desperately to reach agreement, the political tactics they employed, curbing both discussion and elections, affected relationships within the party, and eventually the system of leadership itself.

The system of appointments, begun during the civil war, continued. It was not just one of appointing Bolsheviks to state offices, but also one of using appointments rather than elections to posts within the party. Instead of a party organization electing its secretary, a higher party body would make an appointment to the post. The result was the emergence of patronage networks associated with individual political leaders. If a party's rank and file is not involved in deciding policy positions, and in electing its leading officials, the nature of its relationship to the leadership changes. The ban on factions meant that first the Left, then the Right, Opposition could not, or would not, organize a following at grass-roots level. Unable to identify, in any meaningful way, with a particular political stance, members could do little else but identify with a particular individual (who became a patron, appointing his loyal followers to office) or follow the leadership uncritically. In turn political leaders needed a loyal following, prepared to vote without question when the occasion arose. The reward they could offer for loyalty was promotion. The 1920s, then, saw the emergence of groups within the party identified with a particular individual, the development of what are called patron–client relations. At the top of the party the holding of an office which gave an individual the power to make appointments influenced his ability to get the necessary backing for policy decisions in the key bodies—the Central Committee and the Party Congress. And the individual who was amassing this power more successfully than anyone else was Stalin, in charge of the party Secretariat. Stalin, the card-index Bolshevik, as he was sometimes referred to at a time when it was still possible to make jokes about the General Secretary.

These political developments created a situation in which the leader was in a very strong position to call the troops to order behind him and, as we saw, by the end of the 1920s, new troops were there and anxious to follow. There was a General Secretary and a General Line, the correct path had been found and, it followed, should not be queried. However, a system of patron–client relationships provides an insecure basis for power. Followers will desert if the leader cannot provide the rewards or guarantee their safety, or if another can offer more. Somehow the leader must convince everyone that he, and only he, is the rightful leader. What can he then do? First, he must weaken or remove any rivals. Second, he must obtain a *personal* commitment to himself, the individual, and substitute a belief in his infallibility for a mercenary loyalty. When his followers die on the battlefield, or in a labour camp, with his name on their lips, the leader has authority indeed. But was not this meant to lie with the party? Given, however, the inability of a collective leadership to find the one correct way forward, the task had devolved on to the leader, who in turn jealously guarded his position. But if a leader has the task of discovering the true, the only way forward, he must be superhuman. If identifying the scientific laws that govern the creation and progress of socialism depends upon one man, he must be an extraordinary individual indeed. Stalin emerged as a huge figure standing above the whole system. Stalin the all-wise, the all-knowing, responsible for details great and small. A speech by Kaganovich, a member of the Politburo, describing, in 1935, the building of the Moscow Metro gives us an example of the rhetoric of the time.

The question of our Metro begins from the time when the question of municipal services was discussed at the Plenum of the Central Committee of the Communist Party. The preparations for the discussion of this question of the Plenum were made under the direct guidance of Comrade Stalin. The question of correcting the current defects of our municipal services in the matter of water supply, heating and urban transport has grown into a fundamental question, the question of reconstructing our proletarian capital. It was at this period, while I was making my preliminary report to Comrade Stalin on the practical problems, that Comrade Stalin spoke of the necessity of building an underground railway in Moscow. When I asked him when construction should begin Comrade Stalin gave as he always does, a clear and business-like reply: 'Construction must begin *immediately*'. *Loud applause* ... Comrade Stalin is a man of many affairs. He has the guidance of the whole country in his hands. He goes deeply into the problems of national defence, the problems of industry, agriculture and transport. But I can tell you from my own experience that Comrade Stalin cherishes a particular love and shows particular concern for the problems involved in the reconstruction of the city in Moscow, and in particular the construction of the Metro and the Moscow–Volga canal. He goes deeply into all details of our construction work, how the pavements should be laid, how the roads should be paved ... how schools should be built ... He frequently told us to see to it that the Metro is of high and exemplary quality. Every one of his suggestions served to arouse and to mobilise Moscow Bolsheviks to fight still more stubbornly for the construction of the Metro and for the high quality of the work put into it. If we have succeeded it is only because the construction of the Metro was under the loving and attentive eye of the colossus of our great country Comrade Stalin. *Loud and prolonged applause.*

There are other ways for a leader in a Communist Party system to maintain his undisputed position—family loyalty, very careful juggling of subordinates, and keeping any contentious items off the policy agenda—and a cult will not work without a committed following. That seems to be a necessary ingredient, and a reason why the Brezhnev cult failed, something we shall come back to. But two things are certain: the leader's most dangerous enemies are his colleagues, and public discussion and criticism of the party's policies will undermine its claim to knowledge of the best way forward.

The Stalinist system can, therefore, be summed up as follows. First, there was a huge state apparatus consisting of centralized bureaucratic institutions, responsible for different aspects of activity—economic, social, and cultural—operating on the basis of commands from above, and competing with each other for resources and jurisdiction. Second, one of these, the NKVD, the wielder of coercion, played a major role as executor of policies. Third, there was the institution of the party, the possessor of political authority, the body intended to provide leadership, control the state apparatus, and encourage participation from below, but quite unable to carry out these impossible tasks. The requirement that it discover the correct policy meant leadership conflict, resulting in a winner-take-all solution, and the creation of a superhuman leader; attempts to control the state apparatus, including the NKVD, resulted in a party apparatus identifying with different institutional interests, and a leadership which, viewing with dismay the 'bureaucratization' of its lieutenants, struggled to find ways to re-create that vanguard party. Industrialization and collectivization, however, had meant that the party had taken control of all resources, and thereby created an administrative system which had no place for such a party; it had fought its final great campaign.

The Leninist political arrangements henceforth would be enmeshed in a state-owned, centrally planned economy, and such a combination would be said to constitute 'socialism'. New recruits to the Communist Party, whether in Russia, in Europe, or the Third World, would learn that the definition of socialism was 'state ownership of the means of production plus the leading role of the Communist Party' and, furthermore, that the only way to achieve socialism was to follow the path, first struck by the Soviet Union: priority to heavy industry, collective ownership of land, and one-party rule. Socialists outside the Communist movement, and from time to time reformers within it, disputed that such a set of arrangements qualified for the name of socialism and, by the late 1980s, even the Gorbachev leadership was anxious to argue that reforms were necessary for the system to earn the name of socialist but, for most of the period in question, the Stalinist concept remained unquestioned in the Soviet Union.

FOUR

Terror

WE now address the most difficult topic of all—terror. Although arbitrary arrest and sentencing, either to death, labour camp, or prison, had featured to a varying extent at different times since the revolution, the years of the Great Purge, 1936–8, stand out as a period during which a wave of terror swept through society. By terror, as opposed to repression, we mean a system, if one can call it a system, of arbitrary and indiscriminate violence employed by the rulers against large sections of the population. In most societies at most times, however repressive the authorities may be, citizens know which actions will result in arrest and sentencing; they know what qualify as crimes. With terror, any such rules go; it is impossible to know how to avoid arrest. The most committed supporter of the regime may be arrested, and the most apathetic left untouched. After 1938 when Stalin called a halt, the number of arrests dropped. They continued up until his death, however, both during the war and after, when thousands of returning prisoners of war and those from the occupied territories joined the camp population. In 1948 the accusations and arrests of leading party figures began again, followed by charges against the Kremlin doctors, but never on the scale of the Great Purge. Our task is to analyse this phenomenon and its consequences. It is not easy, for a number of very different reasons.

In 1934 the XVIIth Party Congress met, the Congress of Victors, at which a victorious party celebrated the success of the first five-year plan and the collectivization campaign. The 2,000-odd delegates elected a Central Committee of 149 but when, in 1939, the XVIIIth Party Congress met, only 59 of those 2,000 were delegates; over 1,000 had been arrested, while 98 members of the Central Committee had been arrested and shot. By 1939 Kamenev, Zinoviev, Bukharin, and other leading party figures, had been arrested, tried, and executed. The revolution had devoured its children, but not only its children. Perhaps 5 per cent of the population was under arrest in 1937/8.

The immediate background was as follows. On 1 December 1934 Kirov, Secretary of the Leningrad party, popular within Bolshevik ranks, and one of the few leaders who established a genuine popular following, stepped out of his office in the Leningrad party headquarters and was shot from behind by a young man lurking in the corridor. The circumstances were very suspicious, as was the timing: Kirov was preparing to move to Moscow to take up a position in the central party Secretariat. Years later Khrushchev was to hint that Stalin, in his desire to see a popular rival eliminated, had been involved but this still remains to be established with certainty. Stalin, however, came immediately to Leningrad to supervise the investigation; the assassin, Nikolaev, was accused of being part of an oppositionist group, and Kamenev and Zinoviev were arrested. Arrests were made in Leningrad. The NKVD was given increased powers of arrest, and sentencing was to be carried out by an NKVD board with a representative of the Procuracy present. Then, however, came a lull. The new Constitution, with direct universal suffrage, was being discussed; discrimination against the sons and daughters of rich peasants or professional people was officially ended; people sent letters to the Central Committee and to the Constitutional Commission with proposals for amendments. Everything seemed calmer, the class war was over, a new society was taking shape.

Then, like a bolt out of the blue, in August 1936 Kamenev and Zinoviev were charged with being part of a Trotskyite conspiracy whose aim was the assassination of leading Bolsheviks. NKVD boards were given the right of execution, and no appeal was allowed. Kamenev and Zinoviev were tried, confessed, and were executed. In their confessions they implicated some leading ex-Trotskyists whose trial, the second show trial, followed in January 1937. It involved Radek and Piatakov, two Bolsheviks who in the 1920s had been associated with the Trotskyist opposition, but had long since supported the Stalinist leadership. They were charged not merely with plotting to assassinate Soviet leaders but also with sabotaging the industrial programme. (Piatakov held a high position in the Commissariat for Heavy Industry, whose Commissar, Orzhonikdze, was found dead in his office, not long after an angry telephone conversation with Stalin.) Sentenced to death, they implicated Bukharin in their testimony. Bukharin was arrested, and in March 1938 came what was subsequently called the Great Trial, the last of the three show trials.

It involved, among others, Bukharin, leader of the Right, Rykov, a respected member of Lenin's government, and Yagoda, Commissar of the NKVD under Stalin in the early 1930s, i.e. leading Bolsheviks who had opposed Stalin at one time or another, other old Bolsheviks who were never oppositionists, and Stalinist commissars. They were charged with plotting assassination, including that of Lenin, with sabotage of the industrial project, and spying for the imperialist powers. The charges had widened. They confessed to their guilt and were executed. Although torture, and promises of their relatives' future safety, may have played their part, we have to remember that they believed, without hesitation, that the Soviet Union was a beacon of socialism for the rest of the world, and that they were part of a historical process that could not but triumph and take mankind to a better future. The party's ability, as history's agent, to take society forward could not be questioned; the party was far more important than any individual and would survive Stalin's leadership. It is worth reminding ourselves too that Western legal specialists, diplomats, and journalists among the audience at the show trials accepted the guilt of the accused. They saw what they wanted to see. How much greater were the influences upon the Soviet population to accept that the defendants were enemies of the people. There were those who stood back, or began to doubt once they were arrested, but others believed the official version.

Accompanying the show trials were the arrest and sentencing of sections of the political, industrial, cultural, and military élite. Article 58 of the criminal code was usually used, under which an individual could be sentenced for any action directed towards the weakening of state power or any action that did not prevent someone else so doing. Not merely sabotage but the intention to sabotage, or the failure to denounce a potential saboteur, were criminal offences. The wording of the article was so broad that it could encompass almost any action or lack of action. People were arrested, then held in detention, some were released after a month or a year, others sentenced, in increasing order of severity, to exile, prison, or labour camp, with sentences ranging from ten years to twenty-five years, or 'for eternity'. Some were executed. There was no right of appeal. In 1937 the Red Army and Fleet, beginning with the High Command and continuing with the officer corps, suffered grievously. The party apparatus itself, at republican and regional level, was hard hit. Khrushchev was involved in the purge of the party apparatus in the Ukraine. Within the state apparatus, the Commissariat of Foreign Affairs and the NKVD itself seemed to be particular targets. Yesterday's prosecutors joined the accused. Cultural institutes, universities, theatre and opera companies, writers and scientists all suffered. From Solzhenitsyn we have the description of an incident out in the provinces, which captures something of the atmosphere of the time:

A district Party conference was under way in Moscow Province. It was presided over by a new secretary of the District Party Committee, replacing one recently *arrested*. At the conclusion of the conference, a tribute to Comrade Stalin was called for. Of course, everyone stood up (just as everyone had leaped to his feet during the conference at every mention of his name). The small hall echoed with 'stormy applause, rousing to an ovation'. For three minutes, four minutes, five minutes 'the stormy applause' continued. But palms were getting sore and raised arms were already aching. And the older people were panting from exhaustion. It was becoming insufferably silly even to those who really adored Stalin. However, who would dare to be the *first* to stop? The secretary of the District Party Committee could have done it, he was standing on the platform and it was he who had just called for the ovation, but he was a newcomer. He had taken the place of a man who had been arrested. He was afraid! After all, NKVD men were standing in the hall applauding and watching to see *who* quit first! And in that obscure small hall unknown to the leader, the applause went on, six seven, eight minutes! ... They couldn't stop now till they collapsed with heart attacks! At the rear of the hall, which was crowded, they could of course cheat a bit, clap less frequently, less vigorously, not so eagerly—but up there with the presidium where everyone could see them? The director of the local paper factory, an independent and strong-minded man stood with the pre-sidium. Aware of all the falsity and all the impossibility of the situation, he still kept on applauding. Nine minutes, ten! In anguish he watched the Secretary of the District Party Committee but the latter dared not stop ... after eleven minutes the director of the paper factory assumed a businesslike expression and sat down ... To a man, everyone else stopped dead and sat down ... That same night the factory director was arrested. They easily pasted ten years on him on the pretext of something quite different. But after he had signed Form 206, the final document of the interrogation, his interrogator reminded him: 'Don't ever be the first to stop applauding!'

While the élite may have suffered particularly badly, hundreds of thousands of ordinary people were caught up one way and another in the mass purge. People were arrested for no better reason than that the local NKVD was determined to be vigilant and find the enemies of the people, or as a result of a denunciation by neighbours or workmates either from conviction, or fear, or to gain another room in the apartment. Again, let us turn to Solzhenitsyn:

A streetcar motorwoman was returning on foot late at night from the car depot; on the outskirts of the city, to her misfortune, she passed some people working to free a truck that had gotten stuck. It turned out to be full of corpses—hands and legs stuck out from beneath the canvas. They wrote down her name and the next day she was arrested. The interrogator asked her what she had seen. She told him truthfully. (Darwinian selection!) Anti-Soviet Agitation—ten years ... A plumber turned off the loudspeaker in his room every time the endless letters to Stalin were being read. His next door neighbour denounced him. (Where, oh where, is that neighbour today?) He got SOE—Socially Dangerous Element—eight years ... A peasant, with six children ... devoted himself wholeheartedly to collective farm work, and kept hoping he would get some return for his labour. And he did—they awarded him a decoration. They awarded it at a special assembly, made speeches. In his reply, the peasant got carried away. He said, 'Now if I could just have a sack of flour instead of this decoration! Couldn't I somehow?' A wolflike laugh rocketed through the hall, and the newly decorated hero went off to exile, together with all six of those dependent mouths.

Now for analysis and explanation. The more emotive the issue, the more difficult the historian's task. Millions were sent to their death, millions more experienced years of appalling suffering. Can we attempt a sober assessment of the Great Purge? Should we be concerned to do so? In moral terms the suffering of 1 million is no less a crime than that of 20 million, and the political leadership no less answerable. So far most accounts of the Great Purge are moral tales (and that is what gives them their strength and attraction for a Soviet audience) but not good history or strong on analysis, in part because the data have not been available. Solzhenitsyn's *Gulag Archipelago* is a wonderful memorial to all those who suffered, but that is something different from an analysis of what actually happened and who was involved and why. We may decide a literary treatment is best. The task of historians or political analysts, however, is to explain the terror, and that means establishing whether there was a pattern to events, whether certain categories of the population or certain regions were hit harder than others, whether institutional conflict played a part, whether the NKVD was out of control, and how the political leadership, and Stalin himself, fit into the picture. All of that requires careful research, and data. What are available?

In 1938 Stalin referred to a successful operation to cleanse the party of enemies of the people, but neither before nor afterwards was the terror discussed. The arrest and sentencing of individual wreckers, traitors, and enemies of the people was noted in the press, and that was all. There were no data on numbers or individuals arrested, on the labour camps, on executions. Until Khrushchev's Secret Speech in 1956 there was silence on the use of torture, no mention of the possibility that people had been falsely accused. In 1956 Khrushchev suggested that charges brought against many members of the party and the officer corps were unfounded; that something had gone badly wrong then and in the later years of Stalin's rule. Rehabilitations and discussion began, but in the mid-1960s the topic was pushed under the table again. Only after a cautious recognition by Gorbachev in October 1987, on the seventieth anniversary of the revolution, that Stalinist repression should be properly explored, did the topic become one for public discussion in the Soviet Union. This time it was intellectuals, sometimes organized into informal societies, such as *Memorial*, who brought it before a wider public. Rehabilitations, documentary films of the labour camps or of returning prisoners of war, memoirs, and exhibitions all made their appearance. Only at the end of the 1980s did the possibility become real of looking at the archives, of trying to establish with any certainty the numbers and categories of individuals who suffered, the involvement of the personnel of different institutions, and the actions of politicians, including Stalin.

Western historians and analysts, free from the political constraints operating in the Soviet Union, wrestled with the problem of analysis during Stalin's lifetime and after. A major difficulty was the lack of reliable data. Political conviction, moral outrage, and intellectual approach, however, all played their part in producing the different accounts. Some scholars took census and labour-force data and tried to calculate population losses, including deaths from collectivization, and numbers in labour camps; others relied upon unofficial sources. They came up with very different figures, ranging from 5 to 20 million, for deaths in the 1930s. By the late 1980s Soviet historians began to publish their calculations, which suggested the higher figures may be nearer the truth and now, with the opening of the archives, both statistical and other data will allow for a clearer picture to be drawn.

Both Western and now Soviet writers have turned to personal memoirs in order to fill out the picture, and here there is a problem of a different kind. Memoirs are a tricky source for historians, especially when they cannot be corroborated, and they need to be treated with particular caution when they refer to events or individuals at the top of the political hierarchy. When reading the accounts of the Great Purge, or of Stalinist politics more generally, we need to ask ourselves how good the evidence is and, rather more difficult, if we are justified in using unverified evidence when there is little else. Some will probably turn out to be true, others not. Memoirs are a good source for atmosphere and everyday life although, even then, the reader must be sensitive to the problems surrounding the writing of them. To write an account, whether of arrest and camp life from which one returned, or of an existence not scarred by arrest, must involve most authors in a difficult conversation with his or her conscience and memory. What are truthful accounts in circumstances such as these? Rather differently, the memoirs are written, as memoirs usually are, by the intellectuals, the educated. We have none written by peasants, by workers, or by the criminals who formed a large part of the camp population. Perhaps this gives a skewed picture of the impact of the Purges, and of the way the period was perceived by society as a whole. If we had peasant memoirs would they be preoccupied with the savagery of collectivization, followed by a period of peace and calm, before the Second World War disrupted families and farms once again? When we learn that the NKVD policed hundreds of miles and many rural settlements with a staff of two with motorbikes and no telephone, we have to ask what the Purge meant in the countryside. Perhaps the famine of 1932–3 scarred a generation of peasants, while the Purge did the same for the urban population? We still know very little of popular perceptions, or indeed of social actions at the time. The degree of active involvement in attacking and persecuting those identified as enemies seems to have been far less than in China during the period of the Cultural Revolution, a campaign which has some similarities with that of the Great Purge.

An example will help to demonstrate the difficulty of studying this period. You are interviewing an elderly woman, now in her eighties, about life at the time of the Great Purge, and you have already established that she lived in a communal apartment, in which ten families shared a kitchen and bathroom. Should you ask a seemingly straightforward question 'how many people did you know who were arrested in 1937?', the response will probably be one of wide-eyed amazement, 'Haven't you read Solzhenitsyn? Don't you know that *everyone* was arrested?' If you continue with: 'But were any members of your family arrested?', there may well be a pause ... 'Well, no, not in my family, but everybody else was.' Then you ask: 'How many people were arrested in the communal apartment you lived in?' There's a very long pause, followed by 'Well, hm, I don't really remember, but yes, yes there was one, Ivanov, who lived at the room down at the end, yes, now I remember.' From here you might move on to ask about the office she worked in, and gradually build up a picture of her environment, but this is still a long way from being able to disentangle her views of today from those of the time, or of the more general picture. Even when the events are far more recent, the problem of perception is still present. In the late 1980s, Okudzhave, a singer from the sixties, was asked, at the end of a lecture at the House of Scholars in Leningrad, 'How do you evaluate Stalin?' and replied 'Stalin was a murderer'. According to one person who was present the majority of the audience applauded, whereas another reported the great majority sitting silent with stony faces.

Soviet historians will surely find it even more difficult than their Western colleagues to separate moral and political from historical judgements. It is such an emotive issue, and tied up with the larger question of reassessing the Soviet period as a whole. Prevented until recently from discussing Stalinist repression and terror, now with access to horrific data, and in an environment where even the achievements of Bolshevism seem to be turning to dust, the historian faces an extraordinarily difficult task. How can we explain what happened? As yet, I would argue, we do not have a satisfactory explanation, nor can we until we have better sources. We can, and should, advance hypotheses, try to identify what we need to know, and assess critically the explanations on offer. Let us briefly consider three contrasting explanations, chosen because they are based on different assumptions of what causes political actions. First, there is the one offered by Khrushchev in his Secret Speech. This relies on the role of the individual: Stalin the individual, the suspicious, paranoid personality who could not countenance rivals, is portrayed as the evil genius responsible for the persecution. The only other characters are again individuals, corrupt members of the NKVD, who played to Stalin's paranoia. The implication is that all that happened was a consequence of Stalin's personality; we need look no further into the environment, the political system, or the past in order to understand the Purges. It is individuals, and in this case morally corrupt individuals who make history.

Very different assumptions underlie Solzhenitsyn's *Gulag Archipelago*. According to him, the Purges stemmed from Bolshevik or socialist ideology; terror was a consequence of the success of the October revolution, and 1936–8 was merely one in a series of waves of repression. How was this so? First, Solzhenitsyn argues, because if one believes that class origin determines behaviour and consciousness, if one believes that individuals' actions and ideas are determined by their social origins and that therefore members of the bourgeoisie cannot but act in a particular way, it is only logical to argue that they should be eliminated. Second, he suggests, the strand in socialist thought which believes in reforming criminals or anti-social elements through labour, or socially useful work, encouraged the setting up of labour camps; and, third, the belief that revolutionary justice should be administered by those with a proper proletarian consciousness, and little else, allowed the riff-raff and sadists of society to staff the penal institutions. With industrialization, these ideas were increasingly realized in the system of forced labour and extermination in the camps. The Purges can be attributed to Bolshevik ideology and the weakness of the Russian intelligentsia in not opposing socialist ideas.

Here then is an explanation which sees ideas as determinants. In contrast Swianewicz, a Polish economist who also spent time in the camps, offers us a 'materialist' explanation. He argues as follows: an advanced capitalist economy presupposes, or rests upon, a high degree of economic integration and co-operate effort; at a time of war, it is relatively easy to impose a system of planning upon such an economic system and because it is a time of war the population is willing to co-operate with the government. In the Soviet context, however, the state imposed a planning system upon an economy which lacked the advanced integrating mechanisms and upon a society distrustful of authority. The consequence was that coercion and administrative methods were required in order to create the industrial base. Economic development necessitates the finding of resources for investment, for holding back consumption. How could this be done? One way to reduce consumption was to withdraw consumers from the market, place them in labour camps where they worked and consumed almost nothing. In addition, because this was not a smoothly operating market economy, bottlenecks occurred and an institution was required to shift the labour resources around; the NKVD, via forced labour, distributed the labour force from one sector to another, from the gold mines to forestry, to building the canals. The labour camps, Swianewicz argues, had an economic rationale. By the end of the 1930s they had fulfilled their purpose, the rudiments of an industrialized economy were there but, he suggests, institutions which may come into being for economic reasons do not necessarily disappear when their rationale is gone; it was not going to be easy to dismantle the giant that the NKVD had become, and change an environment of fear and coercion.

I leave it to the reader to consider what the strengths and weaknesses of these authors' accounts are, but a question that has to be addressed head on is that of the relationship between the Leninist political system and terror. Was it inevitable, as some argue, that terror followed from the creation of the Leninist political order which then developed into Stalinism? My answer would be that it was not inevitable, it was not a necessary consequence, but that the Leninist system was one whose features disposed it towards violent crises, to coercion running riot, and to arbitrary violence. Its elements were such that it was prone to ideological convulsions and political violence, in the same way that it had a tendency to produce a leadership cult. Which elements were the relevant ones? First, there was a coercive apparatus, emboldened and enlarged during the industrialization and collectivization campaigns, which, and this is the more important point, was not properly controlled by the political authority because political authority itself, odd as it may seem, was so unstable. The conflict within the leadership and the nature of the party organization tended, as we saw, towards a personalization of power in one individual. The existence of a powerful coercive apparatus, and one leader, claiming the mantle of authority, is a dangerous combination. Furthermore, this was a system whose leaders believed that society shared a common interest, and that once socialism was built, conflict would be no more; this made it extremely difficult to define the criteria for opposition, to think in terms of rules and recognize opponents, because there should not be any. In such a context, opponents became 'enemies of the people'. There were, therefore, both structural and ideological features which made unchecked repression a real possibility; its turning into terror in the late 1930s still awaits its historian.

Now for the political consequences, first those in the short term. If, by the mid-1930s, the party had laid claim to control over all society's resources and, by so doing, found itself entangled in a huge administrative control mechanism and increasingly subordinate to an individual leader, it was still the dominant political institution whose officials' voices overrode those of any others. The Great Purge meant that this was no longer so. The NKVD could question decisions and arrest party officials at will. A question we then have to ask is whether, at a time like this, the notions of rule, authority, and control can be applied at all. Perhaps the dislocation created by the system of terror was so great that it is difficult to talk of a political system functioning in any coherent way. Perhaps we should think in terms of one type of regime in the urban centres, another in the countryside, and yet a third operating in the labour camps, and recognize that we misunderstand the nature of the system if we think of it as a monolith. To put it another way, did Stalinist terror break up political control over the key resources and further reduce the power of the central institutions to influence social activity?

It is difficult to say because the war came, a war which brought chaos on the western front, had the population on the move again, this time to the east, and saw the collapse of the collective farm system in parts of the country. It left 20 million dead and homeless, and the western part of the country devastated. The years following were unbelievably bleak. The population moved back, and rebuilt the economy in conditions of great physical hardship, and fear of the NKVD. What, then, were the long-term consequences? It is a very difficult question to answer. Survey data suggest that by the late Brezhnev period young people were less fearful of the KGB than their parents, which might be evidence that terror casts a long shadow over those born under it, but there was little difference in their behaviour. It would seem that KGB surveillance and political control were sufficient to intimidate most, whether or not they had experienced Stalinist terror. We do not know what the social consequences were. Some of today's intellectuals are convinced that the nation's 'genetic pool' has been irretrievably damaged, a suggestion that most Western social scientists find hard to accept.

Of more immediate relevance today is the question of whether the NKVD and KGB archives should be opened in their entirety. Bakatin, appointed as head of the KGB after the attempted coup in August 1991, argued on television in September 1991 against such a policy. He referred to the little dossier that he had found in the archive on the arrest of his grandfather, which gave the names of those involved. What, he asked, if people learnt that their father, or their mother, or grandparents, had died as a result of a denunciation by the parents of their best friend? What would the consequences for social and personal relationships be if involvement with the NKVD and KGB from the time of the Great Purge until the present became open knowledge?

In the summer of 1991, I was having supper with a regional party secretary in a provincial city, someone who as a modern languages student, fencing champion, and sprinter, had married the PE instructor before going into teaching, then moved into Komsomol work, and up the party apparatus. It was clear as she talked about her life that, in a provincial city, all the élite, political and academic, went to school together and knew each other. At one point in the evening, her husband said, 'I want to show you something', went to the bookcase, and, with his hands trembling and his voice shaking with emotion, brought the dossier he had collected on the arrest and execution of his father. He had been a boy of 4 at the time, and his father, a former Red Army soldier, had worked in the post office. He had never known what had happened to his father because his mother had been too frightened to tell him, and only now, over the past two years, had he managed to collect the relevant papers. There were the names of the people whom his father, under interrogation, had implicated as being in the conspiracy with him—and, in signing his own death warrant, his father had been signing theirs too. What would happen in a city like that, if all those dossiers were opened? There are those who argue that everything must be told, and others who feel that to hold people responsible for what they did then, or later, will do nothing for the present or the future but open old wounds and inflict new ones. It is not an easy question to decide. A rather different one, and again one to which there is no obvious answer, is whether knowledge of the past is important for the building of a political future.

FIVE

Khrushchev and Party Rule

BY the early 1950s a new political élite occupied the positions of power in the ministries and the party. Many of these men had cut their teeth in the crash course of industrialization and collectivization, risen as a result of the Purges, fought through the war, and then employed the policies and methods learnt in the 1930s to rebuild the heavy industrial and military sector—albeit under the watchful eyes of the NKVD and of the suspicious and ageing Stalin. Both Khrushchev and Brezhnev were of this generation. The young Gorbachev was studying law at Moscow University, and active in the Komsomol.

In March 1953 Stalin died. The most senior members of the Politburo (or Presidium of the Central Committee, as it was called at the time) closed ranks, and shared out the key offices between themselves. They were wary and uncertain: how would the population react to Stalin's death? They issued an order that there was no cause for panic, but only in some of the labour camps were there disturbances; schoolchildren wept. In a manner common to autocratic regimes, the new leadership declared an amnesty for some serving sentences for criminal offences, announced price cuts, relaxed the restrictions on private plots, and held a ball in the Kremlin for Komsomol activists.

The ten-year period that followed Stalin's death was important in two respects. First, it witnessed the reassertion of political power over the means of coercion and, second, it thereby put back on the table the question of how a system of one-party rule could or should be maintained. Terror and the war had both upset the system; now, it seemed, it could be put to rights. The party became the dominant institution *vis-à-vis* the secret police, army, and the ministries, and it established its control over the economy, and all cultural and social institutions. By doing so, however, it placed before itself the old problems: how was the authority of a vanguard party to be maintained in practice? How was the relationship between the political and other spheres of activity to be delineated when the party was responsible for everything? First, however, there was the problem of leadership, and of the secret police. We begin with these.

Initially Malenkov assumed both the First Secretaryship of the party and the Chairmanship of the Council of Ministers, the state body, as Stalin had done, but then relinquished the party Secretaryship. This was subsequently given to Khrushchev, the most junior of the leading politicians, which tells us something of the party's lost prestige in the preceding years. Beria remained as head of the MVD, the Ministry of Internal Affairs (in 1948 the commissariats had been renamed ministries), Molotov remained as head of Foreign Affairs, and Kaganovich assumed responsibility for heavy industry. Almost immediately, as we might expect, conflicts emerged within the leadership over policy— towards the economy, agriculture, and foreign affairs. Although in name a collective leadership, there was no sense in which one could think of it as a cabinet, working together, united around a policy programme. On the contrary policy positions became identified with individuals, and individual standing within the leadership became a crucial factor in policy-making.

During the period 1953-7 the arguments and the power play went back and forth. The key developments were as follows. In 1953 all combined against Beria, head of the MVD; he was arrested, shot, and the MVD brought under political control. Malenkov, meanwhile, advocated an economic policy which laid greater emphasis on consumer durables (thus querying the Stalinist law that heavy industry had to grow faster than light) but no change as far as agriculture was concerned; Khrushchev defended heavy industry, but opened up the question of the almost total neglect of agriculture. Malenkov introduced the idea of peaceful coexistence with capitalism rather than the inevitability of war, but was opposed by Molotov. By 1955 Malenkov, although still in the Politburo, had lost on economic policy and been compelled to resign from the Chairmanship of the Council of Ministers. In 1956 Khrushchev, in his Secret Speech, placed a much larger question mark over some of Stalin's policies, and spoke of countries' finding their own way to socialism. In 1957 a tussle took place over economic policy in which Khrushchev seized the initiative by proposing the decentralization of the industrial ministries; in June his older colleagues responded by demanding his resignation. He claimed, however, that only the Central Committee, the body formally responsible for electing the First Secretary, could dismiss him and succeeded in calling a meeting at which he obtained a majority. Malenkov, Molotov, and Kaganovich were titled the Anti-Party Group, dismissed from the Politburo, and given lesser jobs in the state apparatus. Henceforth, until his ouster in 1964, Khrushchev created a Politburo which functioned as his cabinet, and of which he was the undisputed leader. In 1958 he assumed the Chairmanship of the Council of Ministers to complement his party office.

The question of leadership was, therefore, decided in a less destructive manner than thirty years earlier. We now turn to the party's relationship with the police. In June 1953, at a Politburo meeting, with army generals at the ready in the ante-room, Beria was charged by his colleagues with employing illegal means of repression, and arrested. Other leading MVD officials were also tried, and executed, and the ministry put under Politburo control. The charges against the Kremlin doctors had already been denounced as false. It was not until February 1956, however, when Khrushchev made his Secret Speech to the closed XXth Party Congress, that the role of coercion and of the Ministry of Internal Affairs became a topic of public discussion. In making the speech, Khrushchev had several objectives: to undermine the power of the MVD, to restore the party's confidence and its dominance within the system, and to establish the present leadership's claim to rule and its right to replace hallowed Stalinist policies with new ones. In line with such objectives, he did not refer to the mass repression but limited himself to speaking of the arrest and sentencing of innocent party members, and of the Red Army staff. The latter was no more accidental than was his mentioning, as one of Stalin's failings, his desire to play down the generals' role in achieving strategic victories in the war. As a politician, Khrushchev was concerned to make sure the army generals recognized him as someone who would give them their due. In keeping with more practical policy considerations, Khrushchev blamed Stalin for being isolated from real life, as demonstrated by his lack of awareness of the way peasants lived and the state of agriculture; he criticized him for the persecution of national minorities within the Soviet Union, and, in the foreign field, for breaking with Tito of Yugoslavia.

A basic assumption underlying Khrushchev's line of argument was that up until 1934, i.e. after the industrialization and collectivization campaigns had been carried out, the policies pursued by the leadership had been correct, and that it was only with the period of the cult of personality, somewhere in the middle of the 1930s, that things began to go wrong. In other words, according to Khrushchev, the socialist base had been laid in a proper fashion. Yezhov and Beria, the corrupt NKVD chiefs, together with Stalin were responsible for damaging the party but, he insisted, somehow the party had retained its moral self, it was still Lenin's party. Given these assumptions, it seemed only plausible that, with Stalin and the secret police gone, socialism would show its paces. The faults and the errors were due to Stalin and the rule of terror; now the sky was the limit. We shall come back to this optimistic belief, a crucial element in Khrushchev's thinking, when we consider his political blueprint for the new socialist order, but first, briefly, the consequences of the speech.

Its impact was shattering. Some who heard it in the hall fainted, others subsequently committed suicide. The speech was not published. Marked copies were sent down to party secretaries at local level, who read it to closed meetings of party members and then returned their copy to the Central Committee. Not a single one circulated unofficially within the Soviet Union. A translation appeared in the West, either leaked on purpose or by one of the East European Communists, but the Russian original was not published in the Soviet Union until 1989. This tells us something about the environment of the 1950s compared with the 1980s when, in the age of xerox machines and computers, it would be much more difficult to prevent such a document from circulating.

In April 1956 a summary of the main points of the speech was published in *Pravda* in a statement from the Central Committee, which had officially discussed the shortcomings of the Cult of Personality. This was followed by a series of policy measures which further reduced the powers of the MVD. State security was separated out and given the status of a State Committee in the form of the KGB, and a party official put in charge. The labour camps were handed over to the Ministry of Justice, the economic empire of the Ministry of Internal Affairs was dismantled. Amnesties were announced for those sentenced for political crimes, rehabilitations began, and people started to return from the camps. A campaign for socialist legality was initiated.

The years 1956 to 1964 were a period in which an individual's assessment of the period of the Cult of Personality was the key to identifying his or her political stance. Recognizable political positions emerged.

On one side were those who argued that the 1930s were a heroic period in Soviet history marred, unfortunately, by some excesses, but that excesses happen at such times. The domestic and foreign policies of the Stalin period had been correct, and the same general line should be continued. That was the position of the conservatives. The reformers, in contrast, argued that it was a horrific period which still required explanation, and one whose consequences lingered on and should be countered; economic and legal reform was required, and greater cultural freedom. The debate was still under way when Khrushchev was deposed in 1964, and gradually, quietly, the issue was pushed off the agenda, into a drawer which was closed, and kept closed, until the late 1980s.

If, inside the Soviet Union, the speech meant a wind of change, a new cultural climate, and the creation of two bodies of opinion—defenders of the Stalinist past and their critics—in Eastern Europe and within the Communist movement more generally its consequences were more drastic and more immediate. In Poland it triggered off open protests against aspects of Communist rule, and in Hungary a direct challenge that was put down by Soviet tanks. Western Communist parties split, the Chinese expressed their disagreement with Khrushchev's analysis. In his bid to strengthen the party's authority, Khrushchev had perhaps won a temporary victory, but, by denouncing Stalin and some of his policies, he had opened the way for present and future Communists to query the Stalinist dogma that Soviet practices were the only true form of socialism.

In 1961, at the XXIIth Party Congress, Khrushchev returned to the theme and this time the Congress proceedings were broadcast over the radio and in the press. He talked of the wider purge and, implicating his erstwhile opponents, Molotov and Malenkov, in the arrests, asked the rhetorical question: should not those responsible perhaps be brought to trial? No action followed, nor was it clear whether Khrushchev meant it seriously. If, as we suggested in the previous chapter, it was still a difficult issue to face in the 1980s, how much more so in the early 1960s when so many active in politics, including Khrushchev himself, had been involved in the repressions. At the Congress one of the delegates, an elderly woman who had known Lenin, reported that Vladimir Ilich had appeared to her the night before in a dream and said that he did not feel comfortable lying in the mausoleum next to Stalin. A decision was taken to remove Stalin's body, and that night he was secretly buried in

the Kremlin wall. *Pravda* published a poem by a young poet, Yev-
tushenko, in which he referred to elderly Stalinists, tending their roses,
but waiting for an opportunity to return to power. And it was at this
time that *One Day in the Life of Ivan Denisovich*, Solzhenitsyn's short
story, was published. He had sent the manuscript to the editor of the
most famous literary monthly, *Novy mir*, who took it directly to
Khrushchev, who authorized its publication. From these two examples,
we can see both the way in which the political authorities were directly
responsible for what happened in the publishing world, and the way in
which literature played a political role. The two were intertwined in a
way that is rare in a society where art and politics operate more independently of each other.

An important question is how different the reform process under
Khrushchev was from that initiated by Gorbachev, and why the one
ended with the entrenchment of the existing system, the other with its
collapse. We shall come to this in the final chapter but, by way of
introducing the theme and getting a sense of one aspect of life under
Khrushchev, let us consider student reaction to political developments
in Leningrad during 1961–3. What follows is based upon my observa-
tions, as a student, living in a student hostel, and studying in the law
faculty. There was enormous interest in what was being said, whether
at the Party Congress, in articles, or memoirs; we read everything that
came out from artists, writers, and old Bolsheviks about the Stalin
period, and about the present. *One Day in the Life of Ivan Denisovich*
was unobtainable, unless one had a subscription to *Novy mir*. In the
public library, the reader had to ask at the librarian's desk for the copy,
sign for it, and then sit at a table in front of the desk to read it. The edges
of the pages of the story were already black, and the journal simply fell
open at the appropriate page. There was a performance of Byron's *Don
Juan*, not perhaps the sharpest of political satire, but it was staged by a
liberal theatre director who, at the beginning of the preview, brought
on to the stage the elderly woman, dressed in black, who had translated
it from English into Russian, by memory, during her twenty-five
years in solitary confinement. The student audience clapped every
stanza. The renaming of Stalingrad as Volgograd caused disagreement,
though, because of its wartime connotation. There were poetry readings too, but there were no student demonstrations, nor any political
meetings. Such actions were unthinkable. Nor would we discuss political questions except in the open air and with close friends. As a student,

or an ordinary citizen, we were very much aware of being part of an audience, observing the actions of élite members of society engaged in a struggle in which it was very risky to participate. Isolated incidents did occur. There was a seminar one evening in the literature department on the theme of 'Fathers and Sons', a famous theme in Russian literature, in which the discussion got 'out of hand', and a few students criticized faculty members for the part that they had or had not played during the period of the Cult. A participant had written down the discussion, and a copy circulated secretly; I read it, knowing that the individual who had lent it to me would be in serious trouble if it was found out. It did not take very much, even in the period of de-Stalinization, to fall foul of the authorities. An acquaintance had just returned from three years in a labour camp, as a consequence of quoting the line from *Hamlet*, 'Something is rotten in the state of Denmark', at a student discussion in 1956.

In September 1991, in a discussion with students of the history faculty in Archangel, a city in the north of Russia, one of them asked whether discussion and the press were less free in Leningrad in 1961 than in 1991. With a sense of shock I realized that he had no conception of the environment of the early 1960s, and probably none of that which existed before *glasnost* set the media free. The present generation of students, then, is in a qualitatively different position from that of their parents; they have no memory of a period in which censorship existed nor any experience of political repression.wi But the students of 1989–91 were little disposed towards political activity. The absence of punitive constraints has not produced a generation interested in politics; even as observers, they are less interested than were their parents. The attempted coup galvanized a few into action, but only temporarily. There is now a generation who has no political memory of repression and blanket censorship; this sets them apart from all their elders, but with what consequences it is hard to say.

To return, however, to the Khrushchev period. It was still a period in which the boundaries of what was permissible were defined absolutely by the discussion going on above. The political leadership, including Khrushchev, was very clear that it was its role to define acceptable discussion and activity. It was not up to social groups, or individuals, to push the boundaries wider. This feature of the system, connected with the unacceptability of political opposition, was not questioned, but it poses problems for a reform-minded leadership convinced that some changes are necessary. Such a leadership has no way of coping with developments of which it disapproves, other than by banning them. A long-established, almost knee-jerk reaction of the leadership is to bring the barriers down. We shall come back to this, but let us now sum up the new relationship between political authority and coercion. By the late 1950s the coercive organs were under the political control of the party. The use of coercion—surveillance, arrest, and imprisonment—was still an essential element of the system but what was qualitatively different was that each citizen knew what the rules of the game were, what would or would not attract the attention of the authorities. Political rules had been established.

What then was to be the relationship between the reconstituted political authority and society? In the Secret Speech Khrushchev called for a return to Leninism. By this he meant rule by a vanguard party, an élite group making policy and controlling government institutions, ministries, and police through the party apparatus. Full-time party functionaries, they would form a chain of command from the centre to the localities, where, at the grassroots, they would be backed up by a body of committed activists. The Leninist party, that model organization, always aspired to but never realized, would lead society forward. In keeping with his belief in the ability of the party both to inspire and control, Khrushchev attacked the central state bureaucracy, cut down the number of industrial ministries, and put the regional party secretaries in charge of industry. He also engaged in a policy of rapid personnel turnover within the apparatus, bringing in new specialists, and cutting out what he considered to be dead wood. This had all the hallmarks of a strategy employed by the party leadership both before and under Stalin: a stress on personnel as the key resource, an emphasis on the importance of party mindedness, and the commitment to party values by those who were running education, culture, and the legal system. The party is seen as the shock troops, carrying out orders within a system where the objectives are clearly defined. Of key importance is the reliability of the party troops who are responsible, through their power of appointment, for the loyalty of the ministers, generals, judges, university rectors, or editors of newspapers.

It was relatively easy to ensure this aspect of party control. Simultaneously, however, the party had to be able to inspire and lead, through agitation and propaganda, and control of the media. For an organization to be able to do this, however, it has to have a clear sense of its objectives, of the values it is propagating, and its members must share a

commitment to those values. Here the Khrushchev schema ran into trouble: it was not just that the de-Stalinization campaign revealed a party divided between conservatives and reformers but that, by opening the doors again to a mass of new recruits and insisting that now the party should contain representatives of all strata in society, Khrushchev began the obliteration of any distinction between party and non-party members within society. Under Brezhnev the process continued. Although the Brezhnev leadership engaged in a 'review of party cards', as the membership purges were called, and some were expelled, this had more of the air of engaging in a time-honoured exercise than the earlier genuine concern to cut back, quite savagely, and set forth again with a purified membership. The pendulum had swung to the side of mass recruitment and stuck there. This, however, is to run ahead. Here we note that, even in the Khrushchev period, as the party regained its political authority it found it easier to control other institutions than to agree on how to educate and inspire. In the 1920s, despite the policy disagreements, and the expansion and contraction of membership, there was a shared commitment by the members, who felt themselves surrounded by alien elements, to transform social relationships in certain simple ways. That was no longer so.

What of policy under Khrushchev? As we noted earlier, political arrangements which specified a vanguard party encouraged campaigns. A campaign style was part of the system. We find Khrushchev giving special attention to agriculture, an area which lent itself to the traditional campaign strategy. Simple objectives could be set (open up the virgin lands of Kazakhstan, make maize the crop of the future), there was a relatively simple command structure in place (the regional and district party bodies, unencumbered by the complexity that characterized industrial administration), and an appeal could be made to youth, reminiscent of those calls of the early 1930s, to go out and transform the steppes. Some responded. We are not suggesting that Khrushchev's concern with the agricultural sector stemmed solely from its suitability as a campaign area but rather that the type of political arrangements that exist in a society will not merely affect the way policy is perceived and implemented (simple objectives, campaign methods) but that they will *influence* the identification of policy issues, and their appearance on the political agenda. Traces of the concerns that had inspired his generation—equality and 'proletarian values'—still clung to Khruschev. He pushed for an educational reform which would have compelled school-leavers to do two years' manual work before continuing to higher education; in this we see a last flicker of the ideas of the revolution, a flicker which was extinguished by opposition from factory directors, specialists, teachers, and parents.

With his campaign style Khrushchev was harking back to his youth in the first five-year plan period, trying to realize the traditional role of the Leninist party. Simultaneously, however, he was trying to get to grips with the problem of party-rule in a new, state-owned, and administered environment, where the party was closely intertwined with the state apparatus, where its members were drawn from all strata of the new socialist society, and where, it was stated, conflicts of interests did not exist. Was the shock-troop imagery any longer relevant in such a situation? Was it not time for the party, which now contained the 'best representatives' of all social groups, to become more democratic, with more inner-party discussion, and limitations on tenure of office? In keeping with his notion of a society working together to a common future, Khrushchev emphasized the importance of participation by members of society in everyday administration—volunteer patrols to keep order on the streets, comrades' courts in enterprises to impose social sanctions for minor misdemeanours—and the replacement of full-time state 'bureaucrats' by more active soviet deputies. We should note, however, that he did not advocate any changes to the system of appointments (control by the party was essential) nor to the practice of single-candidate elections to soviets. It was for the party to identify who were the best people (they need not necessarily be party members). to act as deputies, trade union chairmen, or judges, and then for the electors to show their approval. He did, however, perceive a need for more open discussion of policy issues, particularly by specialists, as long as it remained within the bounds that the leadership considered appropriate.

A new party programme, and party rules, presented to the XXIIth Congress in 1961, outlined a shining future. The vision and the targets were still there: communism would be built in twenty years, the Soviet Union would overtake the USA in per capita production by 1980, and the difference between town and country, mental and manual labour, would disappear. The state would wither away, but the party would grow stronger. To understand the optimism, we must recognize the strength of Khrushchev's conviction that, with Stalin gone, the Soviet socialist system with its industrial base, which had proved its military ability in the war and was now the leader of a world Communist movement, could fulfil its potential and overtake capitalism. War with capitalism was no longer necessary, economic superiority would win the day. In 1959 Khrushchev accepted an invitation from Eisenhower to visit the United States. His account is revealing on several accounts—of how isolated the Soviet establishment still was from the world outside (neither Khrushchev nor the Ministry of Foreign Affairs knew what Camp David was, and Khrushchev was anxious lest meeting at Camp David implied a snub), and how proud and yet apprehensive he was. There was anxiety initially lest the plane let them down (and Tupolev, the designer, offered to send his son with the delegation as a mark of his confidence), but

All sorts of thoughts went through my head as I looked out of the window at the ocean below. It made me proud to think that we were on our way to the United States in our new passenger plane. Not that we worshipped America ... on the contrary ... No, the reason we were proud was that we had finally forced the United States to recognize the necessity of establishing closer contacts with us ... we felt pride in our country, our Party, our people, and the victories they had achieved. We had transformed Russia into a highly developed country ... I won't try to conceal that subconsciously we had some other thoughts and feelings as well ... You shouldn't forget that all during Stalin's life, right up to the day he died, he kept telling us we would never be able to stand up to the forces of imperialism, that the first time we came into contact with the outside world our enemies would smash us to pieces; we would get confused and be unable to defend our land ...

Khrushchev was impressed by American technology, and agriculture, very impressed, but that in no way shook his belief that the Soviet Union could not shortly match and then outstrip capitalism. The late 1950s were a time of enormous optimism and pride in Soviet achievements. Sputnik went up. The standard of living rose. The reformers felt that socialism had a future.

Accompanying Khrushchev's optimism was impatience when failings occurred. He was baffled when policies and programmes did not work as intended, and frustrated. Despite plans to shift resources to consumer goods' production, the steel-eaters swallowed them up and, even worse, growth rates of both heavy and light industry slowed down. In agriculture, after initial successes, the yields were disappointing. In keeping with the policy of greater specialist involvement in policy discussion, the pages of the press were opened to a discussion of economic reform. For the first time voices were heard arguing that the system of central planning possessed certain in-built problems (lack of responsiveness to consumer demand, and of incentives for new technology), although no one raised the question of ownership. Meanwhile, however, the greater freedom of discussion had produced open conflict in the cultural sphere. The artistic community had split into two: the more traditional writers and artists who tended to be politically conservative against those more critical of socialist realism and of the Stalinist past. Editorial boards clashed, posts as well as art were involved.

Some of the new abstract painters were offered the opportunity to hang their pictures in an exhibition mounted in the centre of Moscow, and Khrushchev was invited, by the more traditional organizers, to a viewing. When he reached the abstract paintings, he exploded, hurled insults at the artists, and swept back to the Kremlin to issue a call for a reorganization of the cultural unions. A meeting was held between Khrushchev and writers and artists at which, in his speech, he struggled to resolve the problem: he made no claim, he said, to be an expert on art, although he knew what he liked, and those with expertise should make decisions, but a socialist government which paid for the education and support of its artists could not countenance works that so clearly did not deserve the name of art. When it came to it, Khrushchev was not prepared to relinquish the party's right (i.e. the political leadership's right) to lay down the truth, in whatever sphere. If opening up debate merely produced unhealthy disagreement, and undermined the notion of all marching in agreement behind a common aim, it was best to curtail it. But what was the common aim and how was it to be achieved? Khrushchev's policy-making grew more erratic and arbitrary as he resorted, in a way that was not new, to making himself *personally* responsible for the policy initiatives. It seemed that only an individual leader could discover the scientific way forward for socialism. And he turned, as Stalin had done before him, to personnel and organization to try to make the policies work. He shifted party and government officials around, sacking, appointing, transferring old and new in his search for the right people; and, in desperation, he reorganized the party apparatus, splitting it into industrial and agricultural committees at regional level and below. He even proposed that members of the Politburo should take responsibility for different branches of agriculture. He failed to realize that they would not follow him blindly. In October 1964 his Politburo colleagues, concerned at his erratic behaviour, and the grumbling in the apparatus, joined ranks and forced his resignation. Faced with a united Politburo decision, the Central Committee fell in line and voted him out. The Khrushchev attempt to make Leninism work had failed.

SIX

The Administrative-Command System under Brezhnev

THE key figures in the new leadership were Leonid Brezhnev, the First Secretary of the Communist Party, Alexsei Kosygin, Chairman of the Council of Ministers, and Nikolai Podgorny, Chairman of the Supreme Soviet or President, the titular head of state. They emphasized that theirs was to be a collective leadership; there would be an end to Khrushchev's hare-brained schemes, his rash erratic intervention in the economy and in politics. One of their first measures was to restore to the party its traditional structure, and to stress the need for the stability of personnel. In 1965, albeit in conjunction with an economic reform, the original ministerial structure was reinstituted. In terms of party–state structures, then, the traditional framework was back in place. The political authorities retained their control over the army and KGB (coercion), the centrally planned system remained, as did central control of the media and culture.

Gradually a more conservative, bland, style began to prevail. Khrushchev's claim that the Soviet Union was in the first stages of building communism was replaced by the more measured announcement that it had achieved a stage of mature or developed socialism. Those troublesome questions of the Stalinist past and its legacy disappeared from discussion; literature lost its sparkle, sociological investigation became difficult. None of this happened overnight. Many specialist issues continued to be debated fiercely and, from time to time, critical voices were heard, but by the end of the 1960s a cloak of caution had floated down from the Kremlin and was settling over society.

In several respects, though, Khrushchev's heirs followed his lead. The party apparatus was clearly to be the dominant political institution, and its role in determining policy, choosing personnel, and guiding and overseeing state institutions was emphasized; the policy of increasing party membership was continued, although at a slightly slower rate. The emphasis, however, was very clearly one of the party producing sensible policy, then controlling and monitoring implementation, rather than campaigning, of acting as a vanguard which literally pulled society forward. The civic values became those of stability and patriotism; socialism's virtues became the absence of capitalism's undesirable features—unemployment, inflation, and terrorism—and a new phrase 'the Soviet way of life' suggested that the present was a satisfactory existence. The party's role became one of defending and maintaining the status quo rather than transforming the present according to a blueprint for the future.

But could a political framework that had been constructed around an élite vanguard party of committed followers, ruling by virtue of its knowing what was best for society, and taking it towards that goal, accommodate such a change of function for its dominant institution? Khrushchev had tried to marry old party traditions and practices—targets, campaigns, orders, and personal leadership—with a more representative party, new structures, and more open discussion. The Brezhnev leadership adopted a different strategy: retain the traditional structures and rules of inner-party behaviour, but change the goals to conservative ones. Why should this not work?

Initially, it looked hopeful. With Khrushchev's interventionist, arbitrary style replaced by a more cautious and sensible leadership there was progress on several fronts. Brezhnev continued to give high priority to agriculture: investment rose, schemes of land reclamation were initiated, incentives increased for the peasantry, and output rose substantially. Throughout the 1970s the standard of living continued to rise. It seemed that technology and incentives could solve the problem of low productivity in agriculture. But by 1980 it had become clear that the return on investment was falling steadily. Agriculture was swallowing up resources, with no prospects of being able to maintain an improvement in living standards, while the government, by keeping prices low in the shops, was subsidizing the consumer at huge cost to the state budget. The mechanism of getting the produce to the shops was still one of orders to the farms, of sending out students and workers to help bring in the harvest, of using the traditional administrative methods. Roads and storage facilities were neglected. In 1978 Mikhail Gorbachev, the party secretary from Stavropol, an agricultural region, was brought to Moscow to be in charge of agriculture, but there was little a young and energetic newcomer could do in the Brezhnev entourage.

The economic reform of 1965, which gave industrial enterprises more control over their own production-mix, some flexibilty over wages, and allowed them to put a proportion of profit into their own funds, suggested a move away from detailed central planning and control from above but, by 1968, the reform had failed. For several reasons. First, once back in the picture, the ministries, anxious to defend their institutional interests, clawed back their old powers. They controlled supplies and could reward performance. Increasingly they reverted to their old ways, issuing detailed instructions to the industrial enterprises, and curtailing their freedom of action. Second, there was dissatisfaction from sections of the work-force itself. Economic reform which aimed at shaking out surplus labour, making it in an enterprise's interest to raise productivity by tying pay to work, did not necessarily appeal to workers who would lose out. Nor was management automatically enthusiastic about schemes that might well not last. Then there was the unfortunate example of Czechoslovakia where an economic reform had developed into a quite unacceptable political reform programme which included reducing the party's power over appointments and the media. Troops of the Warsaw Pact ended the Prague Spring, and from 1968 onwards the Soviet leadership refrained from reform at home. For the remainder of the Brezhnev period administrative reorganization and tinkering with incentive systems characterized industrial policy. The consequence was that by the end of the 1970s, with growth rates continuing to decline, the technology gap between the advanced industrial countries and the Soviet Union was failing to close. New products were not coming on the market. Industry seemed to be trapped in a vicious circle of low wages, low productivity, and poor quality output.

In contrast, the military sector, which had priority in terms of resources, could be seen as a success story: the Soviet Union achieved military parity with the United States. It was during the Brezhnev period that the Soviet Union, its diplomats and politicians, and the United States began a cautious co-operation, as befitted the world's two major nuclear powers. The relationship was not an easy one, but it was by now one between equals. The Soviet government had to be consulted on developments in, for example, the Middle East, and was independently making its presence felt in Africa. The cost, however, was a huge drain on resources. The Soviet economy, with a GNP only half the size of that of the United States, had to devote a far greater proportion of its resources to defence if it wished to compete—and it had a larger population to feed. With growth rates slowing down, the prospects for the future began to look increasingly bleak: an even greater share of resources would need to go towards military spending in order to retain parity with the United States. It would not be long before Star Wars would pose an appalling economic threat, quite apart from a strategic one.

The twenty years from 1954 to 1974 were the best period in Soviet (and Russian) history for the ordinary citizen in the Soviet Union in terms of rising living standards, and peace. By the mid-1970s, however, the momentum seemed to go; it was as though the system had run out of steam. Problems began to mount, as growth continued to slow: the health service, education, and housing all began to creak at the seams. Crime and alcoholism increased. Corruption and cynicism seemed more prevalent. And the government simply continued to produce the same policies.

In January 1987, some ten years later, Gorbachev addressed the problem. 'At some point', he suggested, 'the country began to lose momentum, difficulties and unresolved problems started to pile up, and there appeared elements of stagnation and other phenomena alien to socialism.' He drew attention first to the economy where, he said, outdated management methods, rigid attitudes towards property (i.e. the belief that only state property was really appropriate for a socialist society), and ineffective planning prevailed. 'Day to day practical activity was supplanted by decree making, a show of efficiency and mountains of paperwork, in fact a whole system developed that slowed the socio-economic development of society.' As far as the political system was concerned, serious breaches, he suggested, occurred in party ethics, and the behaviour of personnel degenerated: law-breaking, embezzlement, corruption and report padding, departmentalism, parochialism, and nationalism were prevalent. The social consequences were an increase in immorality and cynicism, young people obsessed with consumerism, a rise in alcoholism, drug-taking, and crime. Culture and art stagnated. Why did this happen, who or what was responsible? According to Gorbachev, the leadership was at fault. It had failed to see the need for new ideas; it had failed to develop new concepts, to identify the problems, and to find new measures to deal with them. It had persisted in operating with outdated concepts and had remained blind, he argued, to the serious shortcomings in the institutions of socialist democracy.

Let us concentrate on his argument that the lack of dynamism, the stagnation, was the consequence of poor leadership, that an innovative leadership could have prevented it, and could have produced the ideas which would have resulted in economic progress, cultural and technological innovation, creativity, and change under Communist Party rule. How convincing is it? Certainly there was an ageing leadership which, with its stress upon consensus decision-making, failed to come up with new ideas. In comparison with the Khrushchev or Stalin periods, a collective leadership existed, although by the mid-1970s Brezhnev had emerged very clearly as the leading figure. He preferred, however, to operate in conjunction with his colleagues. In 1977 he added the post of President to his General Secretaryship of the party, thus allowing himself to act, formally, as head of state. Kosygin, however, remained as Chairman of the Council of Ministers and there was a division of responsibility. From this time on the Chairman of the Council of Ministers became clearly identified as responsible for economic policy, and in particular for the industrial sector. What was noticeable, however, was that Brezhnev had learnt from Khrushchev's mistakes. On the one hand, he manœuvred carefully to get rid of any younger colleagues who looked as though they might pose a threat, and replaced them with elderly individuals (the bringing of the 49-year-old Gorbachev on to the Politburo was an exception, but this was towards the end of Brezhnev's life); on the other, he kept contentious issues off the agenda, and thus prevented policy debate from destroying the consensus in the Politburo. He allowed his colleagues to grow rich with the pickings of office, and he appointed relatives to lucrative or powerful positions. He had found, it seemed, an answer to the problem of how to make the First Secretaryship secure: maintain the status quo—and oppose *any* policy initiatives.

Perhaps most interesting of all though, as far as leadership is concerned, was that by the end of the period the trappings of a cult emerged around Brezhnev. At the final Party Congress, at which his speech could no longer be televised because of his incapacity to read properly, republican after republican party secretary rose to his feet, to deliver accolades to this tireless champion of Marxism–Leninism, creative thinker, philosopher, and statesman. Some of Brezhnev's early writings about Kazakhstan were made into an opera (the steppes, it was said, were alive to the sound of music); more and more medals were pinned upon his chest for his achievements; the posters and pictures become huger and huger. Why did the cult recur? The breeding-ground remained the same: a party ruling by virtue of the fact that it and it alone can identify scientific truths, and the transferring of this impossible claim to the individual leader who thereby has to be wise and all-knowing. But whereas, under Stalin, the cult was for real, people believed that Stalin was all-knowing, and the cult had a social significance, under Brezhnev it was a pale shadow, a mockery. Few people told jokes about Stalin, and not primarily because they were afraid; the jokes about Brezhnev were legion. Perhaps the appearance of a cult that was a source of ridicule should have drawn our attention to the fact that something was badly wrong, that something strange was happening within the political system.

To return, however, to the argument that leadership was responsible for the stagnation. It is correct that the Leninist system was a political system that required an active dynamic leadership if it was not to sink into inertia or something worse; to that extent the Gorbachev analysis correctly identified a key feature. This is, however, not the same as saying that an innovative leadership could have maintained the dynamism. But before considering that, we must look a little more closely at the institutional arrangements between the Communist Party apparatus and the state apparatus in order to show why a dynamic leadership was crucial to the system.

By the state apparatus, we refer to all the institutions that came under the formal umbrella of the soviets, from local soviets, to republican soviets, and up to the Supreme Soviet of the USSR. The Council of Ministers, which included the central, all-union ministries, responsible for all spheres of activity—the different industrial branches, agriculture, culture, education, internal affairs, foreign policy, health—more than a hundred of them in all, was nominally responsible to the Supreme Soviet. The pattern was repeated at republican level, and at regional level the local departments of the different ministries administered the resources that were centrally allocated. All enterprises and institutions were, therefore, under the jurisdiction of one or other ministry, most of which were based in Moscow. During the 1970s, the number of ministries and other central institutions, such as state committees, government agencies, and research institutes, proliferated.

Relationships inside and between institutions seemed to become steadily more bureaucratic in the sense, and here Gorbachev's comments are relevant, of increasing paperwork, documentation, sending instructions down the hierarchy to bodies below, multiplying requests for information from different institutions. A favourite phrase of the time was that all decisions required 'a complex approach'; indeed the perceived need to consult, check, and acquire information seemed to result in a paralyis of decision-making, or to be a substitute for it. The paperwork mounted, administrative orders were issued down complex hierarchies in which no real mechanisms existed for checking their implementation, and each central institution actively defended its own interests. Each claimed that the resources it controlled should be expanded; every ministry, for example, claimed the need for a research institute where specialists could study the complex processes in society and produce new techniques. Ministries expanded, and were subdivided, but then each required extra accommodation and resources. State Committees required reorganization in order to try to coordinate the new more complicated relationships. A spider's web of administrative structures developed, with its centre in Moscow and its tentacles spreading out over the country; millions of employees engaged in processing policies and passing instructions and information to and fro.

Such a huge bureaucratic apparatus, if it was not to act as a brake on change, clearly required a forceful and determined policy-maker standing above it and able to goad it into action. Who was meant to be making policy? Formally the Supreme Soviet, the body elected on the basis of single-candidate elections, was the legislature in the system, but it met only twice a year for a few days to rubber-stamp major legislative proposals. The actual policy-maker was the Politburo, the leading party body, elected, according to the party rules, by the Central Committee but in reality a body whose members were co-opted by the individual (Khrushchev) or group (the Brezhnev–Kosygin team) who had gained control of the key party posts. The Politburo was the cabinet of the system and, by the mid-1970s, its membership had been increased to include the ministers responsible for key policy areas (Defence, Foreign Affairs, and the KGB). Its weekly meetings, chaired by Brezhnev, were where all major policy decisions were taken. The Politburo was served by the Central Committee's Secretariat (Brezhnev was General or First Secretary), whose departments, headed by secretaries appointed by the General Secretary, were second only to the Politburo in importance. Most departments had responsibility for a particular policy area; others were concerned with inner-party affairs. Policy advice and personnel appointments were the task of the Secretariat departments, staffed by the top ranks of the apparatus.

Why, then, were the departments not acting in a creative manner, providing new ideas, policy initiatives, monitoring the work of the state apparatus, and advocating the pruning of the bureaucracy? First, because they tended to identify with the interests of the sector for which they were responsible—the party department responsible for the coal industry became a champion of the coal industry while that responsible for health sought more resources for the health sector— there was a natural tendency for party and state apparatus to work together to defend what they saw as the interests of their sector. Second, there was very little personnel change. The same individuals, many of them quite elderly, held the same jobs in the party and state apparatus for ten, twenty, even thirty years maybe. That surely worked against innovation. But there was a third and more important factor as far as the party apparatus was concerned. As an organization its members always looked up to the level above them; each level took its cue from the one above. It was a leadership-dominated organization in which policies were expected to come from the leadership. It was not an institution that was expected to act on its own initiative. If the leadership was not dynamic, or failed to call the troops to combat, no action would come from the party apparatus. It would simply continue with existing practices, maintain the status quo, and defend its position against attacks from above or below.

Party and state officials, whether at central or regional level, worked together to keep the administrative-command system running in the accustomed way. But, as they did so, the system began to degenerate. There was increasing bureaucratization, the clogging up of the command system. Given a lax attitude by the party leadership and the absence of any mechanisms for control from below, party and state officials, the *nomenklatura*, increasingly misused the resources at their disposal, the funds for which they were responsible. As office-holders who controlled economic resources, political posts, and positions in all state institutions, central and regional officials were obvious candidates for corruption and bribery. They could distribute favours and benefits. Furthermore they controlled the media, which could not question their right to dispose of economic resources, power, and privileges. In the Brezhnev period, the potential for the *nomenklatura* to defend and further its interests increased as the party leadership simply let the system run on. It was not just that personnel remained in office but that, when appointments had to be made, long-time deputies stepped smoothly into their previous patrons' shoes and, in the regions, local members of the élite joined a well-known circle.

In the republics too the educational and affirmative action policies to promote the titular nationalities (Uzbeks in Uzbekistan, Tadjiks in Tadjikistan) began to produce new élites who were of the titular nationality. The eleven pre-war republics had grown to fifteen with the incorporation of the three Baltic states—Latvia, Lithuania, and Estonia—and Moldova, part of pre-war Romania. Russia (which itself contained a number of smaller autonomous republics, based on smaller ethnic groups) was the largest, then came the other two Slav republics—the Ukraine, and Belorussia. Georgia and Armenia, small and mountainous, and Christian, were down in the Caucasus; then there were the five Central Asian republics, Uzbekistan, Tadjikistan, Turkmenistan, and Kirgizia, predominantly Muslim, Turkic, or Persian speaking, and Kazakhstan, where more than half the population was Russian. From the middle of the 1970s major corruption scandals broke in certain of the southern republics, and in provincial Russia. In Georgia, the head of the KGB, Shevardnadze, 'the honest policeman', became First Secretary after one such scandal. In 1987 Gorbachev was to report that half the party apparatus in Uzbekistan had been dismissed for corruption. This tells us is that although the system might appear monolithic, Moscow centred, and controlled, under the surface local élites had formed and were becoming increasingly used to acting in their own interests. This entailed defending regional or republican interests against what they perceived as an ineffective and uninspired central leadership, but one which might still intervene in a wholly arbitrary manner.

The existence of such an extensive administrative apparatus, controlling resources and communications, and the lack of policy change from above, had two consequences for social action. First, there were no mechanisms through which social or political problems could reach the public agenda: nuclear accidents, drug-taking, abortions, or racism were non-subjects. Occasionally an issue did break through as a result of the combined efforts of a group of specialists, journalists, and a politically appropriate moment on high. One such issue, and the frequency with which it was quoted tells us just how few other such examples there were, was the industrial pollution of Lake Baikal, the world's deepest inland lake with its priceless natural heritage. Despite the publicity and the statements, however, it was not clear that all pollution was halted. Meanwhile the Aral Sea, as a consequence of an ill-thought-out irrigation scheme, became an ecological disaster and a health hazard for those living near. A group of Russian writers produced novels, in which the destruction of the Russian village and countryside featured, and occasionally an article by one of them, giving a critical account of village life, appeared on the pages of *Pravda*. But nothing followed.

Specialists and intellectuals discussed what they saw as the decay of their society, but even they had very limited knowledge of what was actually happening, both because of the difficulty of engaging in critical research and of raising issues in the press. Thus, even among the intellectual community, knowledge of society tended to be quite narrowly compartmentalized. Issues which had come on the public agenda in the West—racism, feminism—had no place even on the private agenda of Soviet intellectuals. The official line that nationality problems had, in all key respects if not in their entirety, been solved in the Soviet Union meant that there was no opportunity to discuss the existence, and the reasons for, stereotyped attitudes on race, as prevalent among the intellectuals as among anyone else. This situation had the consequence that neither politicians nor people had any clear knowledge of the extent of social or economic problems. In the late 1980s Gorbachev was to confess that the leadership had been unaware of how serious many of them were.

A second consequence was that the social and political organizations, such as the Komsomol, trade unions, or cultural organizations, and the elected soviets, whose membership had originally acted as mobilizers for great tasks, atrophied as mass institutions. Under Khrushchev there had been a faint attempt to make them institutions through which people participated in civic duties but, even there, the flickers of activity that occurred were as a consequence of reformers engaging conservatives in a struggle to strengthen legal rights or had sprung from the leadership calling for a campaign from above. In the absence of either of these activities, the mass organizations simply became adjuncts of the administrative system. The unions participated in discussions of wage policy at central level, and administered welfare and engaged in personnel management. To the ordinary citizen it was clear that, faced with a pension or a housing problem, one went to the local government official, perhaps with a bribe, not to the local deputy because he or she had no power to affect decisions. Membership in and meetings of these organizations became ever more formal and ritualistic.

Back in the 1930s the campaign to build the new city of Magnitogorsk out in the steppe had caught the imagination of a generation. Under Khrushchev the Virgin Lands campaign could still attract and inspire a section of young people, and produce some good songs. In the Brezhnev period the campaign to build BAM, the great new Siberian railway, simply failed to inspire anything approaching enthusiasm. This tells us that an important change had occurred. The party could no longer run a campaign. The party leadership had no message to offer, nothing to inspire and take society forward. Its conservative values of patriotism and stability could not enthuse and unite the party, let alone youth. The following can serve as an example of the extent to which the ideological aspect of the party's work had deteriorated by this time. Thousands of people were still employed by the ideological apparatus of the party and Komsomol to give lectures to audiences throughout society. A woman lecturer, who specialized on political themes, received an invitation from a provincial party committee to lecture at a factory and at the local army base. The army, as she said, always treated lecturers well, providing a good meal and a fee, and she enjoyed talking to young recruits. She decided she would give them her lecture on 'Lenin and the Komsomol' because it usually went down well. But, as she lectured, to the rows of boys, with their close-cropped dark hair and their dark eyes, she could not arouse a flicker of interest. She could not understand it because, as an experienced lecturer, she knew how to speak to different audiences. She tried everything, but to no avail. At the end, she turned in desperation to the commanding officer, in the hope that there would be questions, but he dismissed the class. As they went out, she said to him, 'I can't understand it, why wasn't I getting a response?' To which he replied, 'That is not surprising, they are Kazakhs, and don't understand Russian.' 'Why then,' she asked in amazement, 'was I lecturing to them?' To which she received the answer, 'Oh, don't worry, they learnt what listening to a political lecture involves.' A ritual exercise. By the 1970s activities which had had a meaning had lost them. Grandparents, even those who in their youth had never been politically active or had been critical of Soviet power, made unfavourable comparisons between Komsomol activities then and now.

What did this mean for the most important institution of all, the party? What did it mean to be a party member in the late 1970s? Membership stood at more than 16 million, one in nine of the adult population. Nearly half of those with higher education were in the party. Political criteria for admission had become vaguer and vaguer; overt dissidence of course excluded anyone but, apart from that, it did not really matter. Admission was by invitation on the part of the party organization at each place of work. Its task was to raise its numbers, bring in new members of the collective who were working well, and make sure that there was a membership spread of different occupations, ages, sex, and nationality. An invitation to join could only be refused at the cost of jeopardizing one's career or retention of a job. The party therefore contained staunch Stalinists, Khrushchev-type reformers, political weathercocks, Social Democrats, Russian nationalists, Baltic patriots, and a huge contingent of people who were not interested in politics at all but for whom joining the party was simply an adjunct to a job. Given this, the party's language became emptier and emptier, more and more wooden. What kind of a language or political message could speak to all those different people, unite such a disparate group? There was not one. The old ideology, with its old phrases, was therefore repeated, becoming less and less meaningful, sounding hollower and hollower. Members assembled for the party meeting, some spoke the words, others raised their hands, and then the membership dispersed to talk in different tongues. In the 1920s or 1930s, if we could imagine lifting the roof of an apartment block, the conversations floating up from the families below would have identified the party members among them; by the 1970s, they were indistinguishable.

Solzhenitsyn, who was expelled from the Soviet Union in 1974, after demanding the abolition of censorship, criticizing official policy, and working on the *Gulag*, suggested that in the Khrushchev period 'breathing and consciousness' returned. As we saw, two different political positions began to emerge: with the reformers pushing for change. No really radical views were expressed, nor could they have been, but the fact that alternatives existed was more significant than their content. Discussion could begin. After the reform momentum was halted in the mid-1960s, some individuals began to develop their ideas, which ranged from reform-communism, to an élitist liberalism, to Russian nationalism, and, in defending them, found themselves classed as dissidents and in trouble. Increasingly harrassed by the authorities, they joined forces in defence of human rights and individual civil liberties (over which they could agree) and to help each other when brought to trial. The authorities were far too strong for them, however. It was relatively easy to pick them off, and to prevent circulation of *samizdat* to any but a small circle. By the late 1970s, it was suggested that there were more dissidents abroad than in the Soviet Union. Sakharov, an outspoken and eminent nuclear physicist, had been exiled to Gorky; and few of the younger generation were coming forward. The dissidents' political influence was minimal. Their suppression by the authorities was, however, significant in another respect. It meant there were no recognized political positions which could provide a basis for discussion. Conservatism and repression had its consequences. The ban on discussion, and the shell of official language that became more and more meaningless, produced a fragmentation of views and prevented the emergence of coherent political positions. Social opinion splintered.

In 1982 Brezhnev died. He was succeeded by Andropov, a more puritanical figure, who initiated an anti-corruption campaign, and began to produce more sober assessments of the economic situation. If the Khrushchev period was one of illusions, the end of Brezhnev's was characterized by disillusionment. Whereas the post-Stalin leadership had held a ball in the Kremlin for the Komsomol, Andropov visited a major Moscow factory and spoke of the need to raise productivity before wages could increase. But Andropov was sick and, upon his death in February 1984, was replaced by the already ailing Chernenko. In February 1985, Gorbachev, the youngest member of the Politburo, succeeded to the General Secretaryship. An anecdote told in the Brezhnev period had Stalin, Khrushchev, and Brezhnev in a railway carriage. The train stopped. Stalin put his head out of the window and shouted, 'Shoot the driver'; the train still stood. Khrushchev put his head out, and shouted, 'Rehabilitate him.' The train still did not go. Brezhnev said, 'Comrades, comrades, draw the curtains, turn on the gramophone, and let's pretend we're moving.' Now when Gorbachev came to power an extra line was added: he joined the others, and his contribution was, 'Comrades, let's get out and push.' The question we now address is whether a dynamic, reform-minded leadership could save the system.

SEVEN

Perestroika and the End of Party Rule

WE begin with a question. Could the powerful state system that Gorbachev inherited have continued unchanged? The slowing economy was certainly creating problems, but there is no reason to suppose that the administrative-command system under Communist Party rule could not have retained its essential features for ten, or perhaps twenty years. More than that, given economic decline, must be considered very unlikely. Although such a statement is of doubtful value because it assumes no major change in either the West, the Arab world, or in China, any of which could have had a decisive impact upon economic and political developments in the Soviet Union, it has a point in emphasizing that there were powerful factors working to preserve the administrative-command system. The stability of the Brezhnev system was real enough as long as certain key props remained in place, and these were undermined by a combination of largely fortuitous factors. Without any doubt, action by the Gorbachev leadership was the crucial one. This does not, of course, mean that Gorbachev intended the outcome to be the collapse of central authority and a primitive struggle for control over resources of all kinds. Far from it.

The question then becomes: could the system have been reformed in a gradual and orderly fashion under one central authority? That is more difficult to answer. It is a question which will long preoccupy citizens of the former Soviet Union. For some Gorbachev is a hero because he brought an unworkable and corrupt system to an end, for others, a traitor, because he undermined a stable, ongoing system, which could have reformed itself. We shall approach it by considering the *perestroika* strategy, the Gorbachev strategy that was intended to result in a manageable reform process, and show why it failed. As we shall see, it was extremely unlikely that it could have worked, but the reasons for this are not straightforward.

Perestroika is best understood as a combination of policies put forward by the Gorbachev leadership during the period from the XXVIIth Party Congress in 1986 until the end of 1989, policies intended to produce major changes in the economic and political system. In the economy, the aim was to introduce elements of a market mechanism, and a variety of forms of ownership; in the political sphere, the vision was of a reformed Communist Party, still firmly in control, but a party whose officials both at central and local level would, to some degree, be accountable to elected bodies. Greater freedom of discussion, and scope for autonomous social groups would characterize a society in which party–state institutions no longer owned and managed all spheres of activity. There was never any doubt that the political unit would be the Soviet Union.

It is helpful to ask how the *perestroika* policies differed from Khrushchev's attempt at reform. First, as concerns the economy, the general aim was the same—setting the economy on a path to catch up with the Western economies and now with Japan, and encouraging the introduction of new technologies, all vital for the maintenance of the Soviet Union as a world power. Gorbachev suggested, however, that radical reform was necessary, thus indicating that the measures were to go further than anything previously attempted. In clear contrast to any earlier discussion, the sanctity of state ownership as *the* socialist form of ownership was first queried, and then abandoned in favour of the argument that a combination of different property forms—state, co-operative, and private—was the more appropriate. The centrally planned system came in for damaging criticism, and the necessity of market mechanisms was accepted. Since the 1930s, as we have seen, the state had taken over the management of all economic resources and had provided an extensive state welfare system, and Khrushchev had never doubted that socialism meant the extension of state ownership and state provision.

In the West too, in response to popular pressure after the Second World War, governments had begun to intervene much more directly in the economy, to nationalize industry, and to take on a responsibility for welfare. The welfare state, as a term, passed into popular usage. By the 1970s, however, with the cost of services rising and management of the economy proving more difficult than had been foreseen, advocates of privatization, deregulation, and cutting back the welfare state had gained a hearing. The issue of redrawing the boundaries between state and society, of the state withdrawing, became a key one in liberal democracies, with socialists on the defensive because they had championed the idea of a popularly elected government using the state to redress the economic and social inequality in society. The gaining of universal suffrage had been seen by the labour movement as a way of countering, with political power, the power and privilege that came with wealth and possession of economic resources. It had turned out not to be so. Making political power responsible had resulted in a large state but not an end to privilege and unequal opportunities. The state had shown itself to be too blunt an instrument to redress the wrongs in society, a poor advocate for socialism.

In the Soviet Union, where the identification of socialism with the extension of state power had been greater than anywhere else, the problem was more acute and the issue highly contentious. The new privatizers found themselves ranged against those who took it for granted that state property was the bedrock of a socialist system. The leadership insisted that change was necessary but, as far as policy was concerned, there was hesitation and plain inaction. We do not have the space to cover the zig-zag economic policies of those years; suffice it to say that by 1989 nothing radical had been done in the economic sphere, the old system was still creaking on, and the debate over its future was growing sharper. The conviction, however, that the almost total state ownership and control was what was wrong with the present system influenced the reformers' views of other state–society relations too. It was not necessary, they argued, in fact it was old-fashioned to think that everything should be controlled and organized by the state. If there should be scope for entrepreneurial economic activity, there should also be scope for autonomous social groups. How much, and what kinds of activity, were unclear, but the Gorbachev leadership implied that it was time to adopt a more flexible approach to social initiatives. The principle, whatever is not forbidden is permitted, should be applied rather than only permitting what had been officially sanctioned.

The policy of *glasnost*, of encouraging a greater openness of discussion, accorded with this view. It was prompted by the belief that the airing of opinions was vital for new ideas to come forward, and that the existence of conflicting views was a normal phenomenon in a modern civilized society. In his argument that a pluralism of ideas was an essential attribute of society, Gorbachev went further than Khrushchev. He still insisted that the general framework of discussion had to be socialist but he was operating with a much vaguer concept of socialism, one which, for example, allowed for different types of property. Indeed Gorbachev's views on what Soviet society might look like at the start of the twenty-first century (the revised party programme spoke of creating a modern society rather than stressing anything to do with Communism) were very similar to those of some Western statesmen, and this had important consequences. Given the lack of any clear criteria of what 'socialist' meant, it became transparently clear that it simply meant whatever the political leadership decided was appropriate. To put it another way, it seemed that all that remained of 'socialism', as its undisputed characteristic, was political control under one-party rule. Gorbachev was adamant on this: pluralism of ideas, and some autonomous social activity, did not mean political pluralism. There was no place for competing political parties in a socialist society.

But how were these new economic and social characteristics of socialism to be combined with Communist Party rule? What kind of political reform was required? Before he could engage in any real initiatives Gorbachev, as any new First Secretary, had to secure his position and replace those who would stymy any attempt at change. He was helped by the age, and sometimes senility, of leading personnel and by the awareness even among those in favour of minimal change that, after years of inaction, there had to be some new policies. With great skill Gorbachev edged individuals out, and brought new energetic individuals into the Politburo and Secretariat. They were not all reformers, indeed Yegor Ligachev, a regional party secretary from Siberia whom Andropov had brought into the Secretariat, was to become the spokesman for a conservative opposition within the party, but, by 1988, Gorbachev had a Politburo and Secretariat in which he could command a majority in favour of reform.

During this early period he employed what we can call the classic strategy, the one adopted by Khrushchev (and practised by both Stalin and Mao at different times). This was the natural strategy for a Communist Party leader striving to extricate the party from a system of bureaucratic state administration, and to make it again take up the task of acting as a dynamic vanguard. There was a call for strong leadership,

and for the clearing out of corrupt or old personnel and their replacement by morally and politically sound individuals at all levels. An attack
upon the bureaucratic state apparatus, the ministries in particular, for
being responsible for inertia and policy failings, accompanied an appeal
to the population to join with the leadership in the great endeavour.
During 1985–8 Gorbachev adopted this strategy: a high leadership
profile, a sweeping out of party and state officials, campaigns against
alcoholism and corruption, and targeting the ministries as the
bureaucrats of the system.

There was nothing very new here. The underlying assumption of
such a strategy was that the structural or constitutional arrangements
of the system were sound: that there should be one party leading and
controlling the state apparatus. As long as there was good leadership
and the right people in place then the system should work well, but the
party must avoid involvement in the institutional wrangling and detail
of everyday administration. Its tendency to become so involved had
been a concern of successive leaderships, as witnessed by the repeated
injunctions from on high against the practice of *podmena*, or the party
officials substituting for, or simply taking over, state administration. It
was, however, an inevitable consequence of the constitutional arrangements themselves: if the party was to be responsible for and to control
state institutions, it necessarily interfered and took charge.

Supposing, however, the size of the state and its control over the
economy and society was lessened, and greater scope allowed for private and social initiative? Could not this solve the problem? The party
would have less to interfere in, and less to oversee, and could then play a
purely political role. The eagerness with which reformers took up the
theme of NEP as having been a viable socialist alternative (different
forms of ownership, pluralism of views) suggested that some saw this as
possible. Had not the move to introduce all-embracing state ownership
been the mistake that had produced the bureaucratic administrative-
command system in which the party could not play the role Lenin had
envisaged for it? But let us think for a minute. Although it was true that,
with the extension of state control, the party could not act as a vanguard, what would the party's political programme consist of if the
relationship between state and society were redrawn and state control
reduced? NEP had presupposed moving *on* to socialism; now such
temporary arrangements were being offered as the model of a desirable
society. If that was so, what did one need the party for? The basis for its

legitimacy was that, as a vanguard party with a mission, and committed followers, it was able to plot the path for the transformation of society, and lead it forward to socialism. Without such a goal, there was no basis for its claim to the right to rule.

In 1988 all the key elements of the system were still in place. Society's response to *perestroika* had differed in certain respects from reactions to the Khrushchev reforms. Little happened in the economic sphere, and the official approval of new co-operative ventures in agriculture met with a minimal response. Nor did anything change in inner-party relationships. *Glasnost*, however, produced a different response from that following Khrushchev's authorization of the airing of certain forbidden themes. The first voices to be heard were those of writers and intellectuals who had been young, and some of them active, during the Khrushchev period. Indeed it was this generation, the children of the XXth Party Congress as they were dubbed, who became the inspiration behind, and the champions of, the *perestroika* policies. Having seen their adult professional life constrained or stifled during the Brezhnev years, they had nothing to lose by a final commitment to reform. They were prepared to speak out, far more critically, on economic, social, and political issues; to vote the conservatives off the boards of the various professional and cultural unions, and, as editors, to introduce a new style of lively and critical journalism. The Politburo authorized the screening of films (such as *Repentance*), made earlier but never shown, and Trotsky appeared on stage. The writers and journalists were still conscious that they owed these new-found freedoms to the political leadership, and they thought in terms of a system in which politics and the press went together. In the spring of 1988, in Gorbachev's absence abroad, an article appeared in one of the more conservative newspapers, *Sovetskaya Rossiya*, which read like a manifesto for a return to the old well-trod paths, and an end to the damaging criticisms of the Soviet past and present. It was clear that it had backing from within the Politburo, and indeed it was from Ligachev. The press fell largely silent. The reformers failed to mount a counter-attack until, three weeks later, *Pravda* came out with an official criticism of the piece, and all breathed again.

If, in this respect, the response was largely similar, other developments were different. Unlike in the Khrushchev period, young people did not go to organized poetry readings and listen to scratchy tape-recordings of Okudzhave, but expanded their pop groups and the range of activities, from ecological concerns to youth clubs, that had begun to emerge in the early 1980s. The freer atmosphere allowed them to express their frustration with local authorities who put obstacles in their way, and a pioneering television programme brought an outspoken and critical youth face to face with officials. Television played a crucial role in breaking down the official public language—whether it was in giving young people a voice or, for example, screening, live, a discussion at a factory meeting of candidates for election as director. In general, though, old ways and words held sway. The new phenomena were still the exceptions, and were recognized as breaking the rules. When in 1987 students in Leningrad demonstrated against the demolition of a historic building, the Angleterre Hotel, they were arrested, and the demolition went ahead. Protests or demonstrations were few and far between, and very quickly suppressed by the police and security forces. But far more clubs, groups, and associations of one kind or another, an alternative culture, were coming into being, and some of these, in Moscow and Leningrad, were concerned with economic reform and with the political issue of Stalinist represssion. In these clubs a generation, previously silent, the professional intelligentsia in their thirties and early forties, Brezhnev's children, began to come together.

That Soviet society had changed since the 1950s no one would dispute. Commentators disagree, however, over both the nature of the society and over the role social change played in the transformation of the political system. It is an important question, both because the answer affects our view of the relationship between politics and society during the period from 1917 to the mid-1980s, and because it may influence our thoughts about the future. We shall consider some contrasting views once we have seen what happened, but the reader might like to start thinking about it.

Back to Gorbachev and political reform, however. At the XIXth Party Conference which met in July 1988 to discuss the question of reform within the party, Gorbachev proposed reforms of the soviet or government structures, which inadvertently had the consequence of undermining the party's leading role. Whatever he may have intended, they tore apart the *perestroika* package, and put on the agenda the possibility of a democratic future for the Soviet Union—although, at the time, few either within or without the Soviet Union recognized that they had this potential. The novel and unexpected proposals related to the Supreme Soviet, and its role in the political system. First, Gorbachev suggested, there should be a Congress of People's Deputies, in which two-thirds of the seats should be open to competition on the basis of universal suffrage. Second, the Congress should elect a smaller body from among its members to serve as a Supreme Soviet, to sit for eight months of the year and act as a legislature, discussing, amending, and voting on legislation. Ministers, as government officials, should no longer be eligible for election as deputies and, indeed, their appointment should be scrutinized by the Congress, which would also be responsible for electing the Chairman of the Supreme Soviet, the titular head of state. The Congress should elect a Constitutional Court, with the authority to oversee the legality of any constitutional amendments. The ideas clearly owed a good deal to a separation of powers doctrine, as practised in the United States: the executive should be separate from the legislature, and a third body, the Court, should be responsible for constitutional legality. At this time too Gorbachev emphasized the importance of a legal state, a state in which even the Communist Party would be subject to law.

These reforms were unlike anything proposed earlier in Soviet history. Here was an attempt to combine the party's institutional power and authority with a new basis of legitimacy: electoral accountability. And herein lay a problem. If the party was to retain its power and authority anyway, it was difficult to see what was the purpose of the legislature. In his elaboration of the proposals, Gorbachev made it clear that the party was to remain in charge. The local party secretary, he suggested, should stand for and have to win election to the chairmanship of the local soviet (and what if he did not?), and a third of the seats to the Congress of Deputies would be reserved for representatives of the social and political organizations (the Communist Party, Komsomol, trade unions, professional associations, etc.). The new elected assemblies, it seemed, were envisaged as bodies which would bring more energetic, perhaps reform-minded, activists into the discussion of policy, and make party officials at least aware of popular grievances. There was no idea of a legislature in which competing parties, representing different interests and programmes, would put up candidates, win seats, and either form or control a government. Missing from what looked like a familiar Western constitutional arrangement was any provision for competing parties.

Let us, however, pause for a moment. In the United States and in Britain the legislature has traditionally been a body in which élite sections of society have sought to defend their interests, and have seen their function to be limited to one of exerting control, where necessary, over the executive. The idea that the US Congress or the British Parliament should be democratic assemblies, representative of all opinions within society, is relatively new, as is the acceptance of political parties as desirable phenomena. So should we perhaps see the Gorbachev proposal as one, from a reform-minded section of the élite, for a legislature, representative of élite elements in society, but able to exert a check upon a conservative and unaccountable executive? In other words, as one which Montesquieu and the Founding Fathers, now being quoted approvingly by Soviet academics, would have seen as appropriate? Such a limited and élitist notion of representation was, however, hard to square with either Soviet or current liberal notions of democracy. 'Soviet democracy', whatever the practice had become, was associated with a concept of directly elected assemblies of ordinary people who took decisions and then carried them out (checks and balances were unnecessary) while, in the West, 'democracy' meant univercusal suffrage and competing parties.

Not surprisingly the proposals were greeted with a great deal of scepticism: here was another administrative rearrangement, elections would be overseen by the party, and little would change. They went through an obedient Supreme Soviet, and preparations began for elections to be held in March 1989 to the Congress of People's Deputies. Initially the election campaign aroused little interest. The electoral commissions still lay in party hands and in many constituencies only one candidate was nominated. At some nomination meetings, however, heated discussions broke out as candidates were nominated to run against those either from, or proposed by, the party apparatus. Given the lack of clarity in the rules, there was opportunity enough for the local authorities to fix the nominations, but sometimes chance intervened. At a meeting in Leningrad, which the party apparatus hoped would result in the single name of a key party official on the list, an elderly man made an impassioned plea for the nomination of a young engineer, Iurii Boldyrev, a party member supported by an unofficial 'democratic' organization in the city, on the grounds that this was the last chance society had to introduce democracy, and collapsed with a heart attack. When the news of his death reached the meeting, Boldyrev's name was included, and he subsequently won the election. Sakharov, whose exile in Gorky had been ended by Gorbachev, was

included among the deputies from the Academy of Sciences after an outcry at his exclusion. In Moscow, Boris Yeltsin, the *bête noire* of the Moscow party apparatus, stood despite official opposition. Yeltsin, regional party secretary in Sverdlovsk (originally Ekaterinburg), a city in the Urals, had been brought by Gorbachev to head the Moscow party, and onto the Politburo. Energetic, outspoken, quick to dismiss subordinates, and with corruption and privilege as his targets, he antagonized party and city officials. When he vented his anger and irritation on Politburo members, and then raised the matter inappropriately at a Central Committee meeting in 1987, Gorbachev resolved that he was more trouble than he was worth. His resignation as Moscow secretary took place at a meeting of the city apparatus at which he was publicly hounded and humiliated; Gorbachev was present and, although discomfited, made no attempt to save him. He took up a post in the construction industry but, already seen by some as a 'real' reformer, was persuaded to stand in the 1989 election. His campaign meetings brought a degree of debate and competition into the political arena which had not existed before. His calls for an end to the special privileges and his attacks upon the party apparatus, his ability to establish a rapport with a crowd, and the campaign waged against him by the authorities, made him the people's hero in Russia.

Although in many constituencies the electorate turned out as usual and voted an unopposed candidate or a party secretary in with a massive majority, Yeltsin swept in, and the phenomenon of important party secretaries losing to little known individuals or failing to get the required 50 per cent of the vote sent a shock wave through the system. In Leningrad, Soloviev, the First Secretary of the Regional Party Committee and a deputy member of the Politburo stood unopposed. It never entered his head that he could lose. When the result, together with others that were damaging for the city party élite, came out, there was a stunned silence from the party headquarters, while the voters realized that the elections were, after all, for real. The subsequent campaigns for the undecided seats (the 50 per cent rule meant that a large number went to a second round), came to life.

The most important consequence of these first elections was the blow to the party's claim that it spoke for the people. When more than 50 per cent of the voters in a constituency crossed the party secretary's name off the ballot, both the claim and the apparatus's self-image took a knock. The elections were revealing in other ways too. First, the party apparatus did not know how to fight an election campaign; as a ruling party, it had never had to. The huge ideological Goliath of lecturers and propagandists could not counter the campaign tactics of the little Davids, who pasted up satirical leaflets or asked difficult questions at the campaign meetings. The Leningrad party newspaper, for example, gave publicity to its opponents by referring to such leaflets and quoting the questions asked by 'clearly irresponsible elements'. Party activists complained that they could not answer impromptu questions because they had not had time to check back with party headquarters.

The behaviour of the rank and file membership also demonstrated that theirs was a different kind of organization from that of a party in a competitive environment. Most of the candidates who stood, and against each other, were party members. The new Congress of Deputies had a higher percentage (80 per cent) of its members who were Communists than had the old Supreme Soviet. Almost all the 'democratic' challengers to the apparatus belonged to the party. Thinking back to the Brezhnev period, we see that this was not surprising. All and sundry belonged to the party with the consequence that it could not wage a united campaign: its members had nothing to unite around. This meant that the Yeltsin victory was enormously important because it provided an alternative figure around which the emerging 'democratic' opposition could subsequently rally. However, it must be emphasized that although in some places there was an 'anti-apparat', anti-government vote, nothing approaching an alternative programme existed, except possibly in the Baltic republics. Votes registered discontent with apparatus rule, rather than support for something else.

Let us pursue the question of elections a little further. The absence of competing parties affects both candidates' and voters' behaviour. Where there are no competing parties, with candidates clearly identified for the voter, the electorate has to decide how to vote on some other basis. In 1989 there were some 'visible' candidates, i.e. party secretaries, who could be voted against (or for); there were others who had acquired a high public profile, for example two prosecutors who had been active in uncovering corruption in high places. In many instances, however, the electorate simply made choices on the basis of profession or sex: workers and women did badly, for example. As far as the candidates were concerned, most saw themselves not as representing a particular sectional interest, or political position; rather they offered themselves to their constituents as individuals.

At an election meeting I attended in a Moscow apartment block, the candidates were allowed three minutes to outline their programmes and, as was traditional, started by giving their autobiographies. Some never got on to their programmes. A youngish man, who had abandoned a Komsomol career to head a co-operative which bought up apartments and rented them out to foreign tourists, remarked that it did not matter since he was unlikely to get many votes anyway; a professor of physics stated that he would not bother to outline his programme since it differed little from others. A middle-aged woman announced that she would press for better housing for residents, for ending the influx of migrant workers, for more provisions, a special fund for Moscow, more money for hospitals, cleaner streets, higher pensions, and price-linked wage increases: all popular demands, and ones that she saw herself fighting for as an individual deputy. One candidate did present a recognizable political programme: investigation of the Procuracy, greater rights for deputies and for informal associations, and the handing of all religious buildings over to religious bodies. The only issue to arouse debate was that of co-operatives. A middle-aged woman attacked the co-operative chairman for having abandoned teaching the young for the sake of money, and his argument that the taxes paid by the co-operative to the city government were of more benefit than unimaginative Komsomol activities cut no ice with some present. In him, and in one other candidate—an energetic, slightly aggressive, skilled worker with a chequered career of party education, expulsion, problems with the authorities, and a spell working in the Far North, who advocated enterprise autonomy and a free rein for entrepreneurial talent—a new political generation made their appearance.

If the candidates revealed both new and old attitudes, so too did the conduct of the meeting. When a candidate asked if he could speak ahead of his turn because he had to leave early, all semblance of order broke down. The chairman ruled against, but a noisy minority (among whom the worst offenders were elderly intellectual men who shouted through their cupped hands) accused him of being formalistic and undemocratic. Many joined in, on one side or the other. The chairman tried a vote, and unwisely declared that a spotty show of hands looked like a majority; the candidate headed for the microphone, but was shouted down by those who held that following the agreed order was the more democratic procedure; others argued that the order had been decided undemocratically. By then the candidate was putting on his coat to leave, but a young candidate (whose action was subsequently claimed to symbolize the intelligentsia's willingness to sacrifice itself for the people) rushed to the microphone and begged him to take his three minutes instead. Somehow, the dispute subsided, and the meeting continued. To what extent, we need to ask, do 'democractic' practices mean the following of agreed procedures?

But what had happened to the Communist Party? If the 1989 elections had undermined the party's assumption of its unqualified popular support, the Congress itself dealt an even worse blow to its authority. The sessions were televised live across the Soviet Union. Work came to a standstill as, with no holds barred, deputies criticized the government, the KGB, attacked and defended the Afghan war, hounded Sakharov, and brought up nationality issues. Suddenly public political discussion opened right up. The old practice of an official line, carefully agreed speeches, and unanimous approval was gone for ever. This was enormously important. The party's ability to pronounce upon the one, correct, policy for the country had been publicly challenged. Political authority began to slip away from the leading party bodies to the Congress of Deputies, and thereafter the existence of an ever more critical media played a crucial role.

The party's loss of control over parts of the press, and over some television channels, in an environment in which a host of young journalists and TV producers were anxious to try out their skills, and had a free hand, produced a wave of campaigning journalism and television, innovative, sensational, and sometimes irresponsible. The young Leningrad TV producer, Nevzorov, took investigative journalism to new heights (or depths), first in uncovering corruption, and then with his interviews with criminals dying from shot wounds, and by zoning in on a policeman clipping the nails of the corpse of a woman lying in a park; he made full use of his popular following to heighten anxiety over rising crime and to put across an ultra-right, Russian nationalist message. The Communist Party still controlled most of the newspapers through its ownership of publishing houses, presses, and access to stocks of paper, and the contrast between the content of the local media, where the apparatus held all the resources, and that emanating from Moscow or Leningrad was marked. But the provinces received the television programmes, which revealed a party leadership squabbling and unable to compete, in ideas or words, with its very different critics.

By the winter of 1989, when the second session of the Congress was due to meet, it was clear that the party was fighting a losing battle to retain its place as the political authority in the system. *Glasnost* and the elections had resulted in its losing control of two key resources: authority and undisputed control over the media. Discontent among some sections of the apparatus with what they saw as policies that were endangering the achievements of socialism and the Union surfaced in criticism of the Gorbachev leadership, and produced an all but acknowledged split between the conservatives and the reformers. The party held together but, in the face of both public criticism and demands from its own more radical members, the Central Committee voted that the party should no longer be identified in the Constitution as the leading institution in the political system. This opened the way to the legalization of political parties in the summer of 1990, but that was after the republican and local elections.

When, in March 1990, elections took place to the republican parliaments and to the regional and district councils, all seats were open to competition, but still only one political organization, the Communist Party, existed legally. Emboldened by the experience of the past year, those (both party and non-party people) who were concerned to push reform forward faster formed associations of Democrats or of People's Fronts to nominate and campaign for individual candidates. Recognizable platforms appeared in a few major cities in Russia, and in some of the republics, the Baltic states being a key example. In the latter, where by then fully-fledged national independence movements had emerged, the election was a two-party, competitive election in all but name, and the People's Fronts won. There and in Leningrad, for example, where one of the newspapers published a list of the candidates that the Democratic Bloc was supporting, the electors could choose on the basis of a political preference. In most places, however, this was not the case, and party officials, quite sensibly, had decided not to stand. Some results suggested an anti-élite vote (against high-ranking government or management officials) but the picture was very mixed (KGB and police did rather well) and differed between urban and rural areas.

The crumbling of an official truth, in an environment in which there had previously been no opportunity for political ideas to compete with each other, revealed a fragmentation of views, a wide spectrum of political beliefs, and an absence of coherent political programmes. Many of the Democrats were clear that they had an opponent in the party apparatus, and in the emerging Patriots, the nationalist right-wing groups, but were not at all anxious to belong to 'narrow' political parties. As certainties crumbled and beliefs were called into question, people began to search for new answers, and for something with which to identify. Religion saw a revival. And this brings us also to the question of nationalism, which was to play such an important role in undermining the continued existence of the Soviet Union. We deal with it here because of its role as a 'political identifier' and the part it played in displacing the authority of the Communist Party and of any central government.

Nationalism is the belief that the political unit (the state) should be based on an ethnic or cultural community; that people should be ruled by those of the same ethnic group. We have not space to discuss the arguments for and against such a view; suffice it to say that, since the nineteenth century, it has emerged as a political doctrine, with a considerable following in different parts of the world, and at different times. It seems to flare up, sometimes more predictably than others. At the end of 1986 riots in Kazakhstan followed the appointment of a new Russian republican First Secretary; in 1988 Armenians and Azerbaijanis were fighting over the territory of Nagorno-Karabakh, inhabited largely by the Christian Armenians but physically an enclave inside Azerbaijan; in the spring of 1990 Lithuania declared independence and by the summer the assertion of ethnic identity as the basis for either political autonomy or sovereignty was pulling the Union apart.

Should this have been predicted? Some scholars always portrayed the Soviet Union as a prison of nationalities, a powder-keg waiting to explode. In 1990 it did. We shall never know whether thirty years earlier the same would have happened, but we can ask whether there were factors in the more immediate Soviet past and present which could explain why nationalism came so strongly to the fore in the late 1980s. *Glasnost*, and elections, were clearly essential to its expression. The question, however, is whether the consequences would have been the same had these policies been introduced under Khrushchev. If one assumes that people naturally think of themselves primarily in ethnic or cultural terms, and consider that such a community should be the political unit, then the answer has to be yes. Given, however, that people throughout history have not necessarily viewed themselves and political rule this way, the question remains an open one.

At any time in the post-war period, nationalism would surely have had a popular appeal in the Baltic republics which, as sovereign states, with very clear cultural identities, had been incorporated into the Soviet Union at the beginning of the war. It would also have been strong among some of the smaller persecuted nationalities. It is difficult though to make a general claim with confidence. The administrative structures of the Soviet Union had been constructed on an ethnic basis (republics on the basis of major language groups) and thus, inadvertently, had perpetuated or created a national identification. Can we identify any developments during the Brezhnev period that could have encouraged nationalism? New local political élites, the result of affirmative action, had grown used to running their regions or republics, and were increasingly frustrated by the bureaucratic centre; some were apprehensive of a reforming leadership that might threaten their powers and privileges, and of plans for economic reform that could undermine their control over economic resources. Others wished to wrest control away from a central authority whose policies were seen to be damaging local resources and interests. Some were prepared to appeal to their electorate in national terms, in order to establish a new basis for themselves, a republican basis. There were also intellectual élites, anxious to defend language and culture, who were quick to offer national independence as a political solution to a republic's economic and social problems. The distant, alien centre that was Moscow was an obvious target. Perhaps too the example of countries in Eastern Europe winning their independence influenced some.

Why, though, should the electorate be swayed by such sentiments? The success of any political message depends, in large part, on who its competitors for the political allegiance of the people are. In the Soviet Union, in the 1980s, apart from the 'democrat' versus 'apparat' identification, there was little on offer. The Brezhnev period left a wasteland of ideas as its legacy. Long denounced as a negative phenomenon, nationalism stepped forward; it both gave people a group identity and was a way of expressing opposition to the over-centralized existing system. One potential competitor was noticeably absent. In the twentieth century social class has been a powerful forger of group identity, and produced political movements opposed to nationalism. In 1917 the socialist parties found an audience among people looking for a way to identify with each other; in the Soviet Union, in the late 1980s, it was very different.

The official categories of worker, peasant, and intelligentsia had been discredited; no one wanted to listen to the language of class. With the exception of the miners who went on strike in the summer of 1989 in the Ukraine, in Siberia, and in the Far North, and in 1990 set up their own Federation, Soviet workers showed little signs of organized action along class lines. Why was this? Miners in any society tend to live in a tightly knit community, and to recognize their fellows as sharing the same interests, hence their solidarity was not surprising. Other sections of the labour force, however, had serious grievances too. Why, as Communist Party rule has faltered, and with the exception of the shipyard workers in Poland, working-class protest has been so limited still requires an answer. Repressive management may be one reason, another may be the division between skilled labour force with a great deal to lose (not merely jobs, but apartments and social security benefits) and an unskilled element (desperate to acquire urban resident permits). But in other societies, including Russia before the revolution, workers have risked their livelihood. Although not the only reason, the difficulty of finding a language of protest has probably played a part. It is difficult to organize a campaign to 'defend the interests of the working class' against a government which has long claimed that as its rationale.

Nationalism became the medium through which discontent with the centrally planned and politically controlled system could be expressed, and the elections to the republican parliaments in March 1990 provided an institutional framework for it. The results produced majorities in favour of independence in the Baltic republics and Moldova, and during the following months the Ukraine, Armenia, and Russia itself issued declarations of sovereignty and demanded, at the very least, a renegotiation of the federal arrangements. Although the centre of the empire, and identified as such by the other republics, the newly elected Russian parliament was as anxious as some others to distance itself from the central government. Within Russia there were voices arguing that Russia had suffered, more than most it was claimed, from Communist Party rule: its culture, countryside, and religion had been damaged or destroyed. Although the ardent nationalists did poorly in the elections, many of the democrats who saw nationalism as a danger were in favour of a voluntary, rather than a forced, union and for greater rights for the Russian parliament. Yeltsin was elected as its Chairman, albeit by a narrow majority and after a struggle, and the parliament resolved that its laws should take precedence over all-union laws if there were a conflict of interest between the two. It also voted to recognize the Baltic states, something to which the central government was strongly opposed.

By the summer of 1990 a 'war of laws'—conflict over whether authority lay with the centre or a republic—was under way. Political authority was shifting from the centre, the Congress of People's Deputies, to the new republican parliaments. This reminds us that political authority may rest upon very different things: upon rules, traditional acceptance, or the beliefs of the members of a state as to whom they owe allegiance. The Union government continued to insist that the Soviet constitution took precedence; the majority of the citizens of the Baltic states saw rightful political authority to lie with their elected representatives; the Russian parliament struggled to resolve the dilemma.

Now, perhaps, the necessary conditions were present for a democratic order? But it takes more than competitive elections, a free press, and the legalization of political parties to produce a stable democratic order, and to see why this is so we need to look at the role played by those who controlled the other resources of power as political authority became ever more dispersed.

EIGHT

Dispersal of Power

POLITICAL authority had passed from the party to the elected soviets, initially to the Congress of People's Deputies of the Soviet Union, and then to the republican soviets or parliaments, but authority did not mean power. In the spring of 1990 too many important resources lay in the hands of others. The chiefs of the military and the security forces answered to the President. The party and state apparatus, which controlled the economy, still took its orders from the Secretariat and the central ministries which, as we noted, were tightly intertwined at the top and formed closely knit élites at regional level. The party no longer had undivided control over the media and communications, but it possessed the lion's share. The original centralized apparatus of decision-making was still in place: a 'government' over which the soviets had little control.

By the spring of 1991 this was no more. The central leadership was struggling desperately to retain its control over the two resources it had left—coercion and economic resources—and, under challenge from the republics, increasingly demonstrated its inability to function as a government at all. The struggle for power was now for control of *all* key resources—coercion, authority, economic resources, and communications—and the soviets, lacking the ability to back up political decisions with sanctions or to cope with the worsening economic situation, were steadily pushed to one side. During 1991 (a year of revolution?) we observe two processes at work: the disintegration of central control over all resources—as in 1917 power again lay scattered over the face of society—and attempts by the new republican leaderships to establish their power and authority.

In this, the final chapter, we trace this dual process, concentrating on Russia. Although the collapse of the centre affected all, the response in different republics and in different regions varied. In Georgia, as 1991 drew to a close, a popularly elected President was under siege in the capital; in Estonia more than one government had tended its resignation to the parliament; in Tadjikistan the Communist Party remained in power. Even in Russia there were significant differences between regions: in some the Democrats had won, in others the *nomenklatura* had shifted the jobs around but still retained all those that mattered. Moscow and St Petersburg may have been the decisive political actors at key moments but activities there were far from representative of provincial Russia. We begin, however, with the demise of the central government, something which affected all.

The Congress, and the Supreme Soviet, were meant to make the government more accountable. Where, however, *was* the government? Under the old system the Politburo was the cabinet, the key decision-maker. Now, however, Gorbachev, the First Party Secretary, was the elected Chairman of the Supreme Soviet, in permanent session. Still head of state, and chief executive, he now also became responsible for chairing the meetings, involved with agenda, and with votes, in other words acting like the Speaker in the House of Commons. Meanwhile the ministers whose appointments had been ratified by Congress in no way constituted a cabinet operating as a policy-making body; the Council of Ministers was far too large, and had never worked like that. The Politburo still met but its authority as policy-maker was now questionable, its members were divided on policy issues, and it was not appropriate that it should be sending proposals, in its name, to the Supreme Soviet. By the end of 1989 both reformers and conservatives were bewailing the fact that the country had no government.

In March 1990, recognizing this, Gorbachev brought proposals to the Congress for the creation of a new post, the Executive Presidency, similar to that in the United States or France. The President was to be elected by the Congress (although in five years time the election should be a popular one, and the holding of office limited to two terms) to an Executive Office, separate from the Congress and Supreme Soviet; he would appoint a Presidential Council, bring forward legislative proposals, be Commander-in-Chief, etc. A minority of deputies proposed making the election a popular one immediately but this was outvoted, and the Congress voted Gorbachev into office. The creation of the Presidency clearly made sense in structural terms: it produced a legitimate and clearly defined Executive policy-maker.

By now, however, March 1990, the newly elected republican parliaments were about to challenge any central authority. By midsummer the key questions had become the continued existence of the Union, and how to prevent economic collapse.

Could this situation have been avoided? If the question is whether *glasnost*, an elected legislature, and the Gorbachev leadership could have produced economic policies to lift the economy and make a Communist Party government more answerable to the people within the framework of the Union, the answer has to be that, although conceivable, it is extremely unlikely. The constitutional arrangements which failed to provide for any real government accentuated the problem but they were probably the least important factor. Supposing the Constitution had, from the start, provided for a popularly elected Executive Presidency. Could it then have worked? It is very doubtful. On the one hand there were powerful vested interests opposed to economic reform (sections of the party apparatus and within the ministries) and, on the other, why should a democratically elected legislature vote for an economic reform package that would necessarily involve higher prices, unemployment, and welfare cuts? Even the most committed government would have had an uphill fight. Furthermore, the nationality issue was already squarely on the agenda. Although we should be wary of any account that concentrates too heavily on the role of an individual leader at a time like this, it is just possible that, had Gorbachev, backed by a committed, reform-minded government, put economic reform proposals and plans for a looser Union before the Congress in 1989, he would have got the support of reformers and party loyalists who still felt a duty to support their party leadership. But this would have entailed, as a consequence, splitting the party because many within its ranks were bitterly opposed to such policies. This, however, was an idea that Gorbachev was not prepared to entertain because of his conviction that only one party, the Communist Party, was needed.

In 1989 the Communist Party of the Soviet Union had nearly 20 million members. In some republics, notably the Baltic, whole sections were shedding their allegiance to the central party leadership. During the course of the next two years the giant organization began to shrink, ever more rapidly. The mass membership of the politically apathetic just quietly drifted away, ceasing to pay their dues once it was no longer necessary; some of the Democrats, including Yeltsin, left in protest against an organization that showed no signs of yielding up its power

and privileges. By the summer of 1990 the party was openly split between a Democratic platform in favour of democratic procedures within the party and the conservatives who, in Russia, had won the leadership of a newly organized Russian republican Communist Party. The party apparatus looked to Ligachev but dared not revolt against Gorbachev, who continued to insist that the party had a future. By the spring of 1991, as a political organization it was dead, but it still owned vast amounts of property.

In his role as President, Gorbachev adopted the same strategy of compromise that he did as party leader. Throughout 1990 he prevaricated, trying to reconcile irreconcilable interests. He appointed an ill-assorted collection of leading politicians, writers, academics, and party spokesmen of different persuasions to his Presidential Council, with the consequence that it proved useless as a policy forum. In September 1990 he wavered between supporting a radical economic reform programme and a more cautious one and, with his insistence that they be reconciled, prevented any action to remedy an ever worsening economic situation. It was at this point he requested, and was granted, the power to rule by decree—but to no effect: soon he was issuing a decree that his decrees must be implemented. In November 1990 came further constitutional changes: the abolition of the Presidential Council, and the creation of a new Federal Council of republican representatives (which not all attended) and a smaller Cabinet of Ministers, which he appointed. By the end of the year he had antagonized leading reform-minded politicians such as Shevardnadze, the Foreign Minister, who resigned, and had appointed a team of conservative ministers, led by the unpopular Pavlov. This was too little and too late to save his reputation with the stalwarts of the party apparatus, by whom he was seen as a weak, vacillating figure who had betrayed the system and when, in January, he failed either to take responsibility for or to denounce the actions of the security forces in Lithuania he lost any remaining support from the reformers. Too late he put forward proposals for a new Union treaty. By the summer of 1991 Yeltsin had won a decisive mandate as the popularly elected President of Russia, and by August Gorbachev had agreed to sign a new treaty that left the centre with few powers. It was, however, clear to all that the issue of centre–republican power was far from solved, whether over economic resources or arms.

If 1989 saw the Communist Party lose political authority and its ability to control the media, and 1990 witnessed the War of Laws whereby authority was slipped away from any central institution down to the republics, the Property War was only just beginning. If change was coming, those who controlled the resources wished to make sure they retained them. Proposals came from the directors of large enterprises for the turning of the enterprise into a share-owning company, with individual directors written in as key shareholders, and this was authorized by a ministerial ruling. Some achieved it, others were blocked. Ministries began to set up consortia, joint ventures, and commercial banks. The party apparatus, a major property owner, began to shift its resources at both central and regional level. In Leningrad the regional party committee invested 5 million roubles in a new commercial bank, and pursued the idea of buying a TV channel; in Perm, a city in the Urals, the party committee set up a firm (which paid its shareholders dividends) which began to rent out party property including the party hotel (still supplied by the state wholesale network), and based a lucrative taxi service for foreign businessmen on its car pool (using state petrol). Individual party officials left the apparatus and moved into new business ventures with long-term colleagues from the ministries. Meanwhile the shops grew emptier and industrial production declined as supply networks broke down.

We now reach August 1991. The one resource left to the centre, by this time, was control over the means of coercion: the armed forces, police, and security forces. Authority and the media had gone, economic resources were being divided up. From the republics talk was coming of republican armies. If central control and defence of the territory, the key rationale of a state, went, then everything went. The coup was an attempt to prevent the dispersal of the last remaining centrally held resource, coercion, and thus to maintain the central state and its empire. The War of Laws had turned into the Property War and, by August, the struggle for power had reached the essential one, the ability to command the use of force.

In the early hours of 19 August, a group of Gorbachev's ministers, including Yazov, the Minister of Defence, Pugo, the Minister of Internal Affairs, and Kruchkov, the head of the KGB, proclaimed a state of emergency. Gorbachev's health, it was announced, prevented him from acting as President and, given the grave economic and political situation in the country, a State Committee had assumed extraordinary powers. The Central Committee of the party responded by sending out instructions that nothing should be done to provoke disturbances, in other words, to oppose the Committee. Gorbachev was isolated in the President's holiday villa on the Black Sea; television and radio were taken over, and tanks rolled into the centre of Moscow. The coup failed as its members lost their nerve, and Yeltsin acted to rally the democratic opposition. None of the leading Democrats was arrested, the telephone network continued to work, and by lunch-time faxes from the White House, the Russian parliament, were reaching the provinces; by evening Sobchak, the mayor of Leningrad, had appeared on television with a damning indictment of the 'former ministers' as he called them. There was a very tense two days while all waited to see if the security forces or the army would move in to take the White House and the Leningrad City Council. The coup leaders backed down. By Wednesday it was over, and Gorbachev back in Moscow; the members of the State Committee were arrested with the exception of Pugo, Minister of Internal Affairs, who shot himself. Yeltsin's stature rose even higher. He used the opportunity of Gorbachev's appearance at the Russian parliament to humiliate him before a television audience of millions and, with a wicked grin, signed a decree banning the Communist Party in Russia. Shortly afterwards Gorbachev resigned as First Secretary, the party was dissolved, and its assets impounded.

The behaviour of the army and the security forces was crucial. Relations within the army high command, assessment of the reaction of the officer corps, and morale among the troops, all played a part. We know little enough about this crucial institution. From 1990 onwards there was endless discussion of attitudes within the army: would disillusionment and anger with a government that had let Eastern Europe go result in political action from the generals? Would the troops fire upon fellow Russians if so ordered? At the time of the coup, the high command was divided, and Yazov indecisive, but the questions are still pertinent. There is evidence that the security force, the KGB, was no longer the tight, centrally controlled, institution it had been, even in Russia. Regional KGB chiefs had competing loyalties—to the central leadership, or to the Russian—and, in the absence of instructions from the centre (one of the most extraordinary features was the failure of the plotters to issue instructions to their own organizations), they were prepared to wait and see, and then to link their fortunes with Yeltsin. This in no way denies the bravery of those who printed leaflets, joined demonstrations, and signed protests, because they did not know what the outcome would be—and their actions, in Moscow and Leningrad, contributed to the leaders' nervousness—but it suggests the outcome might have been very different with a more streamlined army and KGB command. Had they picked up a thousand or so of the democratic activists in the early hours of 19 August, something which they easily could have done, there would probably have been no defence of the White House. The point is important for two reasons: it indicates that central control over the means of force was already slipping by August, and it reminds us that in a future situation where the security force or army has but one loyalty (to a new republican government) it may have no hesitation in moving fast against potential trouble-makers.

The industrial directors reacted ambivalently to the attempted coup, with some taking steps to ensure there were no protests from their work-force. More important, however, it seems that few heads rolled in consequence. The coup attempt, inadvertently, had the consequence of speeding up the process of dismantling the central ministries and of privatization as the republican governments now claimed control over the resources. It also meant that the Communist Party lost its economic power: the buildings, car pools, higher party schools, presses, and publishing houses passed into the hands of the new republican and city governments.

With the coup's failure, the dispersal of control over the remaining resource, coercion, became a reality. The question of republican independence, the end of the Soviet Union, was only a matter of time; the republics could dictate to the centre. The issue that mattered was control over the armed forces, the security forces, and nuclear weapons, and Yeltsin had already claimed and won the right to participate in appointments. The election of Kravchuk to the Presidency of the Ukraine, which possessed nuclear weapons, a substantial part of the Soviet armed forces, and on whose shore the Soviet Black Sea Fleet was based, followed by the declaration of Ukrainian independence in early December 1991 made the issue an urgent one. The vital question was whether the individual sovereign states could agree on who should control the weapons, and whether relations between them could be maintained without recourse to force. The situation was and still is a highly dangerous one. There is an army without a government, and governments without armies. The *Soviet* high command and officer corps feel no allegiance as yet to any of the new republican governments, and they in turn cannot rely on the loyalty of the military units.

In a swift and quite unconstitutional act, the leaders of Russia, the

Ukraine and Belorussia set up a new Commonwealth which would, at least for the time being, provide a framework for unified control over the armed forces and for discussion of economic links, and invited others to join. Eight did so. The future of the Commonwealth must be very uncertain. It is unlikely, given the economic and political instability within the whole of the former Soviet Union, that anything devised at the end of 1991 will persist unchanged. The issues of weapons and economic resources are necessarily highly contentious. A government which does not control the armed forces on its territory is hardly worthy of the name. The only grounds for optimism are that the present governments recognize that if the conflicts of interest cannot be settled diplomatically, the consequences will be far worse than in Yugoslavia. Perhaps the most remarkable feature of 1991 was that a powerful state should have fallen apart with so little violence. The danger, however, is that 1992 will witness the final stage in the drama: the uncontrolled disintegration of the armed forces.

What, then, of the attempts to build a new political order? During 1990–1 the newly elected parliaments, and their presidents, struggled to establish the civilian aspects of rule and to create effective governments, even though they possessed no force to back up their decisions and had little control over economic resources. Hardly surprisingly, they achieved little. In another respect too they were at a disadvantage. There were no conventions on parliamentary behaviour, political bargaining, or party loyalties. In Russia, by the late spring of 1991, the discussion at central and regional level was of the need to strengthen executive authority, and to limit the soviets' insistence that they discuss matters great and small. Government officials and the public joined in a chorus of criticism of the ineffective soviets. A popular charge brought against the deputies, at whatever level, was that they were inexperienced, amateur politicians. It is true that discussion within the Congress of People's Deputies and the taking of decisions was often chaotic. When sessions of the Russian parliament or city soviets were televised viewers watched with dismay as hours were lost over procedural points, and key issues abandoned for want of a quorum. But was inexperience the problem? A more sophisticated analysis suggested that the absence of political parties was to blame.

The majority of those elected to the Congress of People's Deputies had been supporters of the existing system, many lukewarm towards Gorbachev's reforms, but divided on a number of issues. There was a small minority of more radical deputies with Yeltsin and, until his death, Sakharov as key figures, who formed themselves into an Inter-regional Group of Deputies and had some kind of political identity, but even they found it hard to work together. The deputies divided along all kinds of lines, sometimes supporting, sometimes rejecting proposals. This problem persisted after parties had been legalized in the summer of 1990. In the Russian parliament, where, by 1991, something approaching a two-party division existed, a small majority supported the more radical position (on economic reform, republican rights, and restricting the rights of the Communist Party), spearheaded by Yeltsin, now head of government. These deputies, however, saw themselves in no way bound to support Yeltsin's government on issues they disagreed with, and their opponents refused to consider themselves as an 'opposition'. Not merely were parties with clearly defined policy positions absent from the legislative arena but the idea of operating in such a way was antipathetic to many. 'We must stop seeing each other as political enemies, particularly at such a time of crisis' was a common refrain from politicians in 1991.

A democratic order, however, requires the existence and acceptance of political enemies. Neither in 1989 nor by the end of 1991 had viable political parties or conventions on party competition been established. In the post-autocratic Soviet environment, dozens of small parties (even more fragmented and with smaller memberships than in 1917) emerged. Some attempted to refound the pre-revolutionary parties, the Cadets for example, or monarchist parties, others looked to Europe and created the Christian Democrats, Liberal Democrats, or Social Democrats. In 1990 many of the Democrats, including a Democratic Party of Russia, combined in a Democratic Russia movement. Then there were the different Patriot parties, the Russian nationalist ones, which included *Pamyat* and Fatherland, and the People's Party of Russia. All these, however, periodically split, and regrouped. The Communist Party spawned a United Front of Workers, demanding a return to a Leninist system and, after the party was dissolved, a Communists for Democracy. By the end of 1991 there were still no signs of coherent parties with an organized following. The Democrats were in disarray, now that their main target, the *nomenklatura*, had lost political office and Yeltsin was in power. The *perestroika* Communists were disoriented and lacked a programme; the United Front, although noisy, and linking up with some of the Patriots, lacked any real following.

There was much talk, as there had been ever since 1989, of a Russian nationalist backlash and it was clear that Yeltsin felt he needed to pre-empt any such appeals by stressing that his was a government of all of Russia. Time will tell, but, as of 1991, the Russian electorate had shown itself remarkably unswayed by such appeals. The problem, however, remains: where are the parties going to come from in a society where groups are poorly defined and there is such a fragmentation of ideas?

When systems of rule break down, leaders struggle to retain or regain control over resources, to create some instrument through which they can *rule* (the issuing of decrees is a sign of the weakness of their position, rather than strength), and grow impatient with their own powerlessness. By the end of 1991 Yeltsin had gained unwilling agreement for the postponement of any elections until the end of 1992, appointed his ministers, and regional governors to be responsible for the implementation of policy, and was embarking upon economic reform. As Gorbachev before him, he requested and obtained, grudgingly, the right to issue decrees. In November, on television, he was arguing:

I cannot imagine how one can implement a reform directed at democratization and improvement of life in the future without having power. Vertical power. And we are creating this vertical power now, from the president, and to executive officers, to the very bottom. There should be responsibility. And if somebody does not deliver the goods, he must be answerable. That is the case in any democratic civilized state ... that is why I have asked [the parliament] for the right to appoint local heads of administration. I have appointed him but I shall sack him if he does not implement a decree or a resolution by the government ...

Interviewer: Does it mean you are in the course of replacing the power of soviets and of changing the power system?

Yeltsin: No, no, this is executive power. A soviet is, as it were, a legislative part of power, one branch of power, and this is the executive power which should implement decrees, resolutions and laws adopted by the Supreme Soviet and so on ...

The key question, however, is how much control the elected assembly has over the executive's decisions, whether a strong government means a weak parliament, and vice versa, and if so, which is desirable. It is not only former Communist Party leaders such as Yeltsin who insist on the importance of a strong executive. Sobchak, the law professor from Leningrad University, one of the liberal democratic deputies, has become an authoritarian mayor of St Petersburg. After the coup failed he moved the mayor's office into Smolny, the party headquarters and, arguing that the mayor in any normal city had a newspaper, struck a deal with the editorial board of the party newspaper: *Leningradskaya pravda* became *The Saint Petersburg Chronicle*. He also set up an Economic Council which included leading figures from the city's defence industry, some of whom had held places on the regional party committee, in order to try to devise an economic future for the city. A request from the City Soviet, at its opening session in October 1991, that he report on his mayoral decisions brought the reply:

Therefore I want to say, straightaway, that I shall not be making any report at all. Any attempt to interfere in my actions, including actions regarding property, will be rebuffed by me. I do not intend to share power with anyone and, equally, am not prepared to discuss the question with you, respected deputies.

In trying, in a situation of economic collapse, to create and run a government whose decisions are implemented, even democratic rulers became domineering, and are irritated by their former political allies in the soviets who try to curb their actions. They need a block of support, a solid party behind them, and it is not there. It is difficult to be a democrat and rule. The democratic deputies, in turn, know that Russia needs a government but they also know that power must be checked. What should a democrat do in that situation?

Inevitably we find ourselves making comparisons with 1917, and rightly so because in 1991, as in 1917, a system of rule collapsed. Have we then witnessed a revolution? Why do we hesitate? Is it because we are too close to developments and cannot see the contours of the new? Possibly. Perhaps developments in 1917 looked, at the time, equally inconclusio ve and confusing. Depending on developments in the next few years, we might well change our views but, looking at the events of 1991, there are grounds for hesitation. Where, in Russia, was the evidence of significant action by new social groups that resulted in power passing out of the hands of the old rulers? Would the central government have collapsed had it not been for the challenge from the outlying republics? In Russia political office passed into the hands of a new group of people, the Democrats, who included within their ranks members of the professional intelligentsia (lawyers, academics, engineers) and ex-state and party officials. The government had certainly changed, and the old system of total control had gone. But, argued some, was not a regrouping under way, a merger of the old party-state élite with sections of the professions and new commercial talent which would organize economic and political control in a new but far from democratic way? Yeltsin had appointed his governors, and was ruling by decree; out in the provinces the old élite was reorganizing itself. We might want to call this a revolution—the emergence of a new group in control of key resources—but revolutions involve attempts to construct a qualitatively new order of things, whereas here the social and economic élite remained largely intact. Unlike the revolutions of 1789 or 1917, there was no vision of a new era opening for mankind. The new rulers did not offer grand ideas of a new order but rather dwelt on the need to undo the mistakes of the past.

Are we then, perhaps, witnessing a restoration rather than a revolution? Have the fears of the early Bolsheviks that after revolution comes reaction finally been realized? Trotsky had argued in the mid-thirties that the new stratum of office-holders would aim to consolidate their power by cloaking it with legality. One group within the democratic opposition had argued from 1987 onwards that *perestroika* was an attempt by the *nomenklatura* to transfer its power over economic resources into legal power, jettisoning the outdated Communist Party system which had begun to limit its activities. Privatization, state deregulation in an environment in which democratic control would be weak, chaotic, and confused, would give the apparatus new opportunities for wealth and privilege, and the legal right to pass these on to its heirs. According to such reasoning, the Democrats had been duped by a wily strategist. They won elections to the soviets, and then discredited themselves in the eyes of the population when they were unable to provide any goods at all, thus paving the way for a new authoritarian government once they had carried out the task of privatization. The argument gains a certain plausibility from the fact that such a process may be occurring, but that does not mean it was consciously engineered. It assumes a too far-sighted and united entrepreneurial élite, whereas one of the consequences of Communist Party rule has been a society of groups, weak on self-identity, and poor at defending or furthering their interests. If the forces of revolution seem lacking, so too are those of restoration. Certainly the renaming, the attempts to revive pre-revolutionary cultural institutions, and the insistence that status and rewards should go with culture and talent in a stratified society, all hark back to an earlier past, but, in Russia, there was little left of pre-revolutionary groups or institutions, the monarchists remained very few, and attitudes towards the state's responsibility for welfare, or towards property and wealth suggested a very different society. Neither revolution nor restoration seem appropriate terms to describe what happened in 1989–91.

Conclusion

WHAT does the future hold for what was the Soviet Union? The question is impossible to answer, not simply because it is so uncertain but because there is no one answer. The republics are going their different ways. Violence in Georgia does not mean it will occur in Estonia; political developments in Uzbekistan do not say anything about the future of the Ukraine. They all face economic problems, of varying severity, some are experiencing savage ethnic conflict, and the existence of large minorities of other nationalities within particular republics is a potential source of conflict between them. Suppose, however, they manage to remain at peace with each other, and with the outside world. What are the chances for a future democratic order, for economic recovery, and for a cultural renaissance—in Russia, the centre of the old empire?

Is Russia in a better state now than it was in 1917 to achieve any of those? Let us begin with democracy. We need to know what circumstances are conducive to the creation of a stable democratic order. Some suggest that a democratic culture is required. If this is true, what kind of a society is Russia today? Some scholars have argued that during the past fifty years industrialization has created a literate, urbanized society in which the rigid, repressive system of one-party rule became increasingly anachronistic; a professional middle class emerged, committed to greater political freedoms, and whose ideas influenced a new generation of party leaders. *Perestroika* and the moves towards democracy showed us a political system responding to a society which had acquired the attitudes, aspirations, and culture necessary for democracy. In such a view, Russia in 1917 was not ready, whereas now it is. This assumes that Soviet society has developed certain traits which are common to those of industrialized societies, *in spite of* the political constraints of a repressive political system. Others, however, stress the continuity of pre-revolutionary political and social attitudes. They refer to the continuity of Russian culture, arguing that authoritarian or collectivist beliefs remained despite the attempts to instil a new Soviet culture, and may provide the basis for a powerful anti-democratic political order. Although drawing quite different conclusions, such a view also sees the Communist regime as a shell inside which society continued to live, or to develop, and from which it then emerged to live a new life.

This would be dismissed by those Soviet sociologists who, in contrast, argue that Russian society, in the late 1980s, was the *product* of seventy years of Communist Party rule. Urbanization and industrialization took a different form from that in the West, and with different social consequences; the key features of Russian society are neither a new educated professional middle class with democratic values nor the preservation of older Russian values, neither of which exist, but rather a low cultural and educational level, a high degree of criminality and of marginal groups, and a lack of social cohesion or moral values.

I leave it to the reader to consider these assumptions, and the very different pictures that are given. The evidence to support any of them still needs to be found. Implicit, however, in my account is the assumption that the combination of political and social policies practised since 1917 have produced a society different from those of the industrial West and one that owes little to its pre-revolutionary past. Maybe in some of the southern republics Communist Party rule has allowed the continuation of traditional political attitudes, but in Russia? Think back to 1917. Both professional middle class and working class were more active then, their leaders better educated, they were better organized, and there was a stronger tradition of engaging in a political struggle for democratic rights and freedoms. Collectivist authoritarianism did not dominate then, and democratic values do not owe their existence to industrialization. That much we can say. The evidence there is suggests that Communist Party rule has created a society, weak on élite groups, with a population democratically inclined, opposed to privilege, short on political knowledge and organization, and seeking for new group identities.

A very different approach focuses not on the doubtful presence or absence of democratic values as a key factor for the establishment of a democratic order but on the presence of social institutions: if universal suffrage and competition are suddenly introduced in a dictatorial system, the consequence will be fragmentation, instability, and the search for a strong government to bring order; the existence of well-balanced élites, prepared to bargain and compromise, and to agree to procedures that safeguard their interests are vital for democracy to gain a footing. If that is so, the prospects are not good. But we should not assume that the experience of post-Communist society will repeat that of other post-authoritarian regimes. Again we must recognize how little we know of that society. We can, however, predict that those who control coercion and the economic resources will be in a powerful position to influence future developments, and that political office-holders engaged in constructing a new order at a time when government barely exists will opt for authoritarian measures to try to give their authority substance in policy. The democrats have a task ahead of them.

I leave it to others to answer the question on the economic prospects, but suggest that there is no obvious relationship between economic recovery and democratic practices. In the late 1980s some Soviet writers, thinking of the experience of South Korea and Taiwan, began to advocate the 'iron hand' solution: authoritarian rule and a free market. Others saw the emergence of a new stratum of small entrepreneurs as a building brick for property rights, and thence democratic rights. At least we can say that economic chaos is hardly conducive to creating a democratic order. The influence of politics on art and culture is as difficult to determine. It is too simple to refer to the crippling effect of censorship and leave it at that. Has the greatness of Russian culture and literature owed something to the tension between the political order and the artist, whether under Tsarism or the Communist Party? Is it possible that once the artist is not needed or expected to be society's political and moral voice art becomes less creative?

In conclusion, let us imagine a future generation in a hundred years time, looking back at the period in Russian history from 1917 to 1991. What might they see? Some might view Bolshevism as the final attempt to preserve the Russian Empire, to create a strong state in a modern society which could compete with others; an attempt which failed because society was too poor to support the cost of such an empire in the modern world. How will that leap out of backwardness be perceived? For most of the twentieth century the Soviet experience has been viewed as an alternative to the capitalist way to industrialization;

for those looking back will it, in contrast, appear a misguided and damaging attempt? Perhaps Communist Party rule will be seen as an attempt to realize the twentieth-century belief that government could solve the problem of injustice and poverty, and as the most striking example of the large state of the twentieth century. Or, in contrast, as the first in a new type of politics: messianic, committed, often violent, a new type of order aiming to obliterate distinctions between different spheres of activity—economic, moral, political—a politics which becomes more common in the twenty-first century. Finally, because this takes us back to where we started, perhaps 1917–91 will be seen as the first unsuccessful attempt to realize the socialist ideal of equality, justice, and freedom, an attempt which failed but which will come back on the agenda, not necessarily or even probably in Russia, in the twenty-first or twenty-second century.

Chronology

1917	(Feb.) Abdication of the Tsar; Provisional Government formed.
	(Aug.) Kornilov marches on Petrograd.
	(Oct.) Bolsheviks take power in the capital. Council of People's Commissars created
1918	(Jan.) Constituent Assembly closed down.
1918–20	Civil War.
1921	(Mar.) Kronstadt revolt.
	Xth Party Congress: NEP adopted; ban on factions.
1924	(Jan.) Lenin dies. Triumvirate of Kamenev, Zinoviev, Stalin.
	Left Opposition, associated with Trotsky.
1926	Trotsky expelled from Politburo; Kamenev and Zinoviev in opposition.
1927	XVth Party Congress: decision on industrialization.
1928–32	First five-year plan.
1929	Collectivization begins; Right Opposition, associated with Bukharin; Stalin as leader, General Secretary.
1932	Famine in the Ukraine.
1934	XVIIth Party Congress.
	Assassination of Kirov.
1936	New Constitution.
1936–8	Great Purge; show trials, execution of Kamenev, Zinoviev, Bukharin.
1940	Trotsky assassinated in Mexico.
1941–5	German invasion; Second World War.
1953	(Mar.) Death of Stalin; leadership including Malenkov, Molotov, Beria, Kaganovich, Khrushchev takes over.
	(July) Beria arrested.
1956	(Feb.) XXth Party Congress: Secret Speech.
	(Nov.) Soviet intervention in Hungary.
1957	(June) Khrushchev confirmed as First Secretary; anti-party group expelled from Politburo.
1961	XXIInd Party Congress; new party programme and rules; Stalin removed from mausoleum.
1962	Publication of *One Day in the Life of Ivan Denisovich*.
1964	(Oct.) Khrushchev removed; Brezhnev, Kosygin, Podgorny leadership.

1965	Economic reform; reinstatement of industrial ministries.
1968	(Aug.) Warsaw Pact troops intervention in Czechoslovakia.
1974	Solzhenitsyn expelled from Soviet Union.
1977	Brezhnev becomes President of Soviet Union.
1978	Gorbachev joins Secretariat.
1982	(Nov.) Brezhnev dies; replaced by Andropov as General Secretary of Communist Party.
1984	(Feb.) Andropov dies; Chernenko replaces him.
1985	(Mar.) Chernenko dies; Gorbachev becomes General Secretary.
1986	(Jan.) Yeltsin becomes Moscow Party Secretary.
	(Feb.) XXVIIth Party Congress.
	(Dec.) Sakharov returns from exile.
1987	(Jan.) Gorbachev puts political reform on the agenda at Central Committee meeting.
	(Nov.) 70th Anniversary: Gorbachev advocates re-evaluation of the past.
	(Dec.) Yeltsin dismissed as Moscow Party Secretary.
1988	(July) XIXth Party Conference: Gorbachev proposes electoral and constitutional changes.
	(Oct.) Popular Fronts set up in Baltic republics.
1989	(Mar.) Elections to Congress of People's Deputies.
	(May) Congress opens; sessions televised.
	Gorbachev elected Chairman of Supreme Soviet.
	(July) Miners' strikes.
	(Dec.) Sakharov dies.
	Lithuanian party breaks with CPSU.
1990	(Jan.) Armed conflict between Armenia and Azerbaijan.
	(Feb.) Party Central Committee votes in favour of removing party's right to be the single party.
	(Mar.) Elections to republican and local soviets; victories for Popular Fronts in Baltic republics, and Democrats in certain cities.
	Constitutional change: Gorbachev elected to Executive Presidency.
	Lithuania declares independence.
	(Apr.–July) Declarations of sovereignty from various republics, including Russian republic; Yeltsin elected Chairman by Russian parliament.
	(July) XXVIIIth Party Congress: conflict between conservatives and Democratic platform; no change; resignation of party membership by Yeltsin.
	Legalization of political parties.
	(Sept.) Gorbachev acquires right to rule by decree.
	Stalemate on economic reform.

1990   (Nov.) Constitutional changes: Federal Council and Cabinet of Ministers created.

(Dec.) Shevardnadze resigns.

1991   (Jan.) Conservative cabinet appointed, headed by Pavlov.

Security forces storm Lithuanian TV centre.

(Apr.) Referendum on Union, and on popular election of Russian President.

Miners demand resignation of government and Gorbachev.

(June) Yeltsin wins popular election to Russian Presidency.

Leningrad votes to rename itself St Petersburg.

(July) Discussions between Gorbachev and republican leaders on new Union treaty.

(Aug.) Attempted coup by leading ministers.

Communist Party dissolved; assets frozen. Yeltsin acquires veto over appointments.

(Sept.) Baltic states acquire independence. Georgia declares independence.

(Dec.) Kravchuk wins election to Ukrainian Presidency; declaration of Ukrainian independence. Commonwealth of Sovereign States agreement signed by Belorussia, Russia, and Ukraine; other republics join. Winding-up of institutions of Soviet Union, including Presidency; Gorbachev leaves office; Russian flag flies over the Kremlin.

Further Reading

This short bibliography provides the reader who wishes to pursue the topic further with a variety of books, written at different times, and from different perspectives.

BIALER, S., *The Soviet Paradox* (New York, 1987).

CHAMBERLIN, W. H., *The Russian Revolution*, 2 vols. (New York, 1965; originally published 1935).

CONQUEST, R., *The Great Terror* (London, 1968).

FITZPATRICK, S., *The Russian Revolution* (Oxford, 1982).

—— (ed.), *Cultural Revolution in Russia, 1928–1931* (Bloomington, 1978).

GORBACHEV, M., *Perestroika* (London, 1987).

HOSKING, G., *A History of the Soviet Union* (New York, 1985).

—— *The Soviet Awakening* (London, 1990).

KAISER, D. (ed.), *The Workers' Revolution in Russia, 1917* (Cambridge, 1987).

LEWIN, M., *The Making of the Soviet System* (London, 1985).

—— *The Gorbachev Phenomenon* (Berkeley, Calif., 1988).

LUXEMBURG, R., *The Russian Revolution* (Ann Arbor, Mich., 1961; originally written 1918).

MEDVEDEV, R., *Let History Judge* (New York, 1961).

NOVE, A., *Was Stalin Really Necessary?* (London, 1964).

OGNYOV, N., *Diary of a Communist Schoolboy* (London, 1928).

SAKHAROV, A., *Sakharov Speaks* (New York, 1974).

SCOTT, J., *Behind the Urals* (Bloomington, Ind., 1973; originally published 1942).

SIMIS, K., *Secrets of a Corrupt Society* (New York, 1982).

SMITH, G., *Soviet Politics, Struggling with Change* (London, 1991).

SOBCHAK, A., *For a New Russia* (London, 1992).

SOLZHENITSYN, A., *One Day in the Life of Ivan Denisovich* (London, 1963).

—— *The Gulag Archipelago*, 3 vols. (New York, 1978).

STITES, R., *Revolutionary Dreams* (Oxford, 1989).

SWIANIEWICZ, S., *Forced Labour and Economic Development* (Oxford, 1965).

TALBOTT, S., *Khrushchev Remembers* (New York, 1974).

TUCKER, R., *Political Culture and Leadership in Soviet Russia* (London, 1987).

VLADIMOV, G., *Faithful Ruslan* (London, 1978).

WHITE, S., *Gorbachev and After* (Cambridge, 1991).

YELTSIN, B., *Against the Grain* (London, 1990).

Index